Comfort After Pet Loss Guide

Effectively Cope with Grief, Move Past Denial, Initiate Emotional Healing, Memorialize Your Beloved Pet and Get the Support You Need

Contents

Introduction

L osing a pet is not just an event; it is an emotional journey that can feel as profound and challenging as the loss of a human loved one. I understand this deeply because I have walked this path myself. When my family and I said goodbye to our beloved pet, the void it left in our lives was palpable. Our home felt emptier, and our hearts heavier. It was during this period of profound sadness that I found myself searching for comfort and understanding, not just for myself, but for my family, especially the younger members grappling with such a loss for the first time.

This book is born from those days of searching for solace, for understanding, and for ways to honor the memory of our cherished companion. It is written for you, the pet owner who has experienced the sting of such a loss, who may be seeking guidance on how to navigate this challenging time, and who needs affirmation that your grief is real, valid, and deserves space to be expressed and understood.

The mission of this book is clear: to offer you comfort, to guide you in supporting children through their grief, to explore meaningful ways to memorialize your beloved pet, and to find strength in a community of fellow pet lovers who understand your pain. Unlike other books on pet loss, this guide combines personal insights with professional advice, providing a balanced perspective on handling grief, initiating healing, and celebrating the life of your pet.

You will find that this book caters to a broad spectrum of pet owners. Whether your companion was covered in fur, feathers, or scales, the love you shared transcends species and the grief you feel is universal. Structured to walk you through the initial stages of shock and sorrow to a place of acceptance and remembrance, the book is segmented into thematic parts that address each stage of the grieving process.

Consider this book as your compassionate companion, here to offer a message of hope and reassurance. The path through grief is undoubtedly challenging, but there is a way forward, a way to heal and to hold dear the memories of your pet. I invite you to engage with this content openly and honestly. Allow yourself to fully experience and express your feelings as you read. It is only through acknowledging our emotions that we can truly begin to heal.

This book promises not just to be a source of empathy but also a practical guide. You will find actionable advice on how to effectively cope with your grief, ways to memorialize your pet that resonate with your personal sentiments, and strategies to garner the support you need during this difficult time. Together, let us honor the lives of our beloved pets and navigate the complexities of grief with compassion and understanding, towards a place of healing and heartfelt remembrance.

Chapter 1: The Unique Bond Between Pets & Owners

Have you ever noticed how a room seems to light up when your pet walks in? Or perhaps how your mood shifts, almost magically, when you lock eyes with your cat, or when your dog places its head gently on your lap? This isn't just your imagination playing tricks on you, it's a testament to the extraordinary bond we share with our pets. This connection goes deeper than the joy of companionship; it taps into an emotional and psychological synergy that has evolved over thousands of years. In this chapter, we explore the rich tapestry of the human-pet relationship, delving into the dynamics that make this bond not only unique but also essential to our emotional well-being.

Decoding the Human-Pet Bond: Beyond Companionship

Emotional Connectivity

Pets have a remarkable way of offering unconditional love, a quality that endears them to us in ways that often surpass our human social interactions. This unconditional love manifests in their consistent happiness to see us, their relentless affection, and their unwavering presence in moments of sorrow and joy alike. For many, a pet is not just an animal but a family member whose emotional bond is as complex as any human relationship. The depth of this connection can often be seen in how pets seem to 'tune in' to our moods, offering a nuzzle or a playful gesture just when we seem to need it most. This emotional synchronicity not only enhances our daily lives but also contributes fundamentally to our emotional resilience, providing a buffer against the stresses of life.

Mutual Dependence

Pet relationships are underscored by a profound mutual dependence that blurs the lines between the care we provide and the support we receive. On a basic level, pets depend on us for their survival, food, shelter, healthcare and exercise. Conversely, we rely on them for more than just company; they provide us with emotional support that often acts as a cornerstone for our mental health. This symbiotic relationship fosters a deep-seated bond, knitting our lives together in a shared experience of life's ups and downs. For instance, consider routine daily walks with a dog, while the pet exercises and explores, the owner gains a moment of escape from the daily grind, an opportunity to breathe fresh air and stretch their legs, often leading to lowered stress levels and improved mental health.

Non-verbal Communication

The bond between pets and their owners is also significantly shaped by non-verbal communication. Pets are adept at reading body language and tone of voice, responding to our silent cues in ways that can seem uncannily perceptive. This form of communication transcends the spoken word, allowing pets and owners to interact on an instinctual level. The flick of a tail, the tilt of a head, or the pacing of paws can convey volumes about a pet's needs and emotions, just as our own non-verbal responses communicate to them our feelings and intentions. This dynamic creates a shared language that, while unspoken, forms one of the most genuine forms of communication and understanding. Birds, such as parrots, use non-verbal communication to interact with their owners through behaviors such as eye pinning, feather ruffling, and body posture. They also use beak movements, and tail displays to convey emotions, intentions, and responses, creating a rich, expressive language that is understood by their owners.

Historical Context

Tracing the evolution of pets from working animals to beloved family members offers fascinating insights into the human-pet bond. Initially, animals were integrated into human societies primarily for practical purposes such as hunting, guarding, and herding. Over time, the utility of animals transitioned into companionship, altering the human-animal dynamic significantly. This shift was influenced by changes in societal structure, where the role of animals expanded to meet emotional and social needs, reflecting broader cultural transformations about the value and perception of animals. Today, pets are considered full-fledged family members, with their welfare often regarded as paramount, mirroring the deep emotional bonds that have evolved.

This intricate web of emotional connectivity, mutual dependence, non-verbal communication, and historical evolution sets the stage for understanding just how profound and multifaceted our relationships with pets are. As we continue to explore these themes, the significance of each aspect of this bond becomes increasingly apparent, providing us with greater appreciation and insight into the roles pets play in our lives.

Why Losing a Pet Feels Like Losing a Family Member

The intense wave of sorrow that engulfs us following the loss of a pet is both profound and deeply personal. This overwhelming grief mirrors the anguish experienced after the death of a human loved one, a similarity that may seem puzzling to those who have never formed a deep attachment to an animal. Yet, for those of us who have opened our homes and hearts to pets, the reason is clear: the unconditional love and companionship they provide forge bonds as significant as any human relationship. Each pet, with its unique personality and irreplaceable presence, becomes an integral part of our lives and our families.

Consider the daily routines that are second nature to any pet owner. Morning walks, feeding schedules, cuddling, vocalization, and even the simple, quiet presence of a pet in the room are all threads in the fabric of everyday life. When a pet passes away, the disruption to these routines leaves a palpable void. The silence in the moments where a jingling collar or the soft thud of paws on the floor should be is haunting, a stark reminder of the absence of a cherished companion. The spaces they once occupied in our homes feel emptier, their beds and toys becoming poignant symbols of their loss. For rabbit owners, they cherish and miss their pets' gentle and affectionate nature, along with their playful antics like hopping and binkying. Adjusting to this new reality without their physical presence is a painful reminder of just how intertwined our lives had become.

Pets also serve as a significant emotional support system, often acting as confidants who listen without judgment, provide comfort without conditions, and give us a reason to smile even on the toughest days. For individuals who live alone, this role is all the more crucial. A pet's presence can alleviate feelings of loneliness and isolation by providing companionship and a sense of security. Losing such a companion can feel like losing a lifeline, leaving one to navigate the challenges of daily life without their constant source of emotional support and unconditional love. The impact is similarly profound for those who do not live alone but who relied on their pet for a unique form of companionship that human relationships do not always fulfill.

Beyond the physical presence and daily interactions, the shared memories we create with our pets contribute significantly to the depth of grief experienced upon their passing. From the exciting day you brought them home, through holidays spent together, to simple, lazy afternoons, each memory adds layers to the bond you share. These memories, rich with emotion and significance, become stories we treasure and recount, imbued with love and nostalgia. When a pet dies, it's not just their immediate presence we miss but also the joy of creating new memories with them. Every memory, whether poignant or joyful, serves as a reminder of the depth of the relationship and the gap left by their absence.

Moving past this multifaceted loss presents a profound challenge, one that encompasses emotional, physical, and psychological dimensions. The grief that is felt, mirrors the complexity of human relationships, underscoring the significant role pets play in our lives as companions, confidants, and family members. As we continue to explore the nuances of this bond, the reasons why losing a pet feels so devastating become increasingly clear, validating the profound sense of loss many pet owners experience.

The Science of Grief: How Pet Loss Affects Us

The grief that envelops us following the loss of a pet is not solely an emotional burden; it manifests physically, psychologically, and socially, weaving a complex tapestry of impact that touches every facet of our lives. To fully understand the depth and breadth of this grief, it is crucial to examine the physiological responses, the psychological impact, and the social implications that accompany the loss of a beloved pet. Additionally, recognizing the healing process as an essential pathway through grief underscores the multifaceted nature of recovery, which necessitates time, support, and an abundance of self-compassion.

Physiological Responses

Grief is not just felt with the heart but also by the body. The loss of a pet can trigger a cascade of physical effects that underscore the profound impact of this event. Stress responses are particularly pronounced, with symptoms such as increased heart rate, disturbances in sleep patterns, changes in appetite, and a general state of fatigue.

These are the body's natural reactions to the acute stress of losing a cherished companion, a testament to the depth of the bond shared. Neurological changes also occur, with grief activating the brain's pain pathways, similar to the response triggered by physical pain. This neurological activity can lead to decreased concentration, disorientation, and a sense of cognitive 'fogginess', which many bereaved pet owners have experienced in the days and weeks following the loss of their pets. These physiological responses are not only natural but also indicate the intense stress the body endures during emotionally tumultuous times.

Psychological Impact

The psychological ramifications of pet loss frequently manifest as intense emotions such as sadness, anger, and guilt, and can evolve into more profound psychological conditions like depression and anxiety if not addressed. The bond with a pet is built on daily interactions and unconditional love, and the severance of this bond can feel akin to losing a part of one's self. For many, pets are not just animals but confidants and sources of unconditional support. The absence of this source of affection and understanding can lead to feelings of emptiness and despair, which are common precursors to depression. Anxiety may also surface, particularly around thoughts of the pet's last moments or anxiety about the future without the companionship of your pet. These psychological impacts are significant, validating the need for grief to be taken seriously and handled with care.

Social Implications

Socially, the effects of pet loss are often characterized by isolation or misunderstandings. In many cultures, the significance of a pet's death may not be universally acknowledged, leading to a lack of empathy or support from friends, colleagues, and acquaintances. This can result in the bereaved feeling isolated or misunderstood, compounded by comments that may seem dismissive like "it was just a pet" or "you can always get another one." Such interactions can intensify the sense of loneliness and misunderstanding, driving the bereaved further into isolation. Additionally, the loss of a pet can disrupt social routines, such as those shared walks in the park with fellow dog owners, or rides with fellow horse owners which were not only exercise but also important social engagements. The withdrawal from these activities can further deepen the sense of isolation and loss, underscoring the significant social impact of pet bereavement.

Healing Process

Understanding the healing process in the context of pet loss involves acknowledging that grief is not a linear progression but a journey marked by ups and downs. Healing requires time, patience, and the support of understanding individuals who recognize the gravity of the loss. Self-compassion becomes a critical component of this process, allowing individuals to navigate their grief without self-judgment. Engaging in self-care practices, seeking support from pet loss groups, and possibly professional help are all steps on the path to recovery. It's important for individuals to allow themselves to fully experience and express their grief, understanding that healing is not about 'getting over' the loss but learning to live with it in a way that honors the memory of the beloved pet.

This exploration into the science of grief underscores the profound effects of pet loss, spanning physical, psychological, and social realms. It highlights the necessity for a compassionate approach to dealing with such losses, recognizing the legitimate pain and disruption they cause in one's life. As we delve deeper into understanding these impacts, it becomes increasingly clear that the path to healing is not only necessary but also fraught with challenges that require support, understanding, and time.

The Stages of Grief After Losing Your Pet

Navigating the stages of grief when coping with the loss of a pet provides a framework that can help make sense of the emotions that might otherwise feel overwhelming or chaotic. Elisabeth Kübler-Ross's model, initially conceived to understand grief related to terminal illness, outlines five stages: denial, anger, bargaining, depression, and acceptance. While these stages offer a valuable perspective on human grief, it's crucial to adapt and understand them in the context of pet loss, recognizing the unique emotional landscape that comes with the passing of a beloved animal companion.

In the denial stage, it's common to experience shock or disbelief. You might find yourself expecting your pet to greet you at the door or hear their sounds around the house. This isn't a sign of losing touch with reality but a natural defense mechanism that cushions the immediate blow of loss, allowing your emotions to catch up with the reality of your pet's death at a more manageable pace. During this time, simple rituals such as keeping your pet's bowl in its place can be a gentle way to transition into acceptance of your pet's passing, rather than abruptly removing all traces of them, which can be jarring.

Anger, the second stage, can manifest as frustration or irritability. You might find yourself angry at the circumstances of your pet's death, the vet, or even at yourself. It's important to understand that this anger is a surface expression of the pain of your loss. Channeling this emotion into activities like writing about your pet or engaging in vigorous physical activities can be a constructive way of processing. Writing might include penning a letter to your pet expressing the things you never got to say, while physical exertion, like a brisk walk or run, can help release the tension that builds up with anger.

Bargaining often involves replaying 'what if' scenarios in your mind, thinking about what could have been done differently to prevent the loss. This stage can be particularly painful because it mires you in the past, often with a sense of guilt. To navigate this stage, it might be helpful to talk to someone who understands the inevitability of death, such as a counselor or a vet, who can provide a rational perspective on the situation and reaffirm that you did the best you could for your pet.

Depression in the grief process can feel like a heavy cloak of sadness that is hard to shed. It reflects the reality of living in a world without your pet. This might be the time when you most feel the absence of your pet's presence, and mundane tasks can seem extraordinarily difficult. Creating a memory book or a photo album can be a therapeutic way of honoring your pet's memory and celebrating the time you spent together. This activity allows you to revisit and cherish the good times, providing a sense of peace and acceptance.

Finally, acceptance doesn't mean you no longer feel the pain of loss, but rather that you have begun to find a way to live with it. In this stage, your memories of your pet might bring more smiles than tears. It's a time when you can begin to look back at your time together with gratitude instead of grief. Starting a new tradition in your pet's memory, such as an annual donation to an animal shelter on their birthday, can be a meaningful way to honor their life and the love they brought into yours.

Each person's experience of grief is deeply personal, and not everyone will experience these stages in a neat, linear fashion. Some might skip stages entirely or experience them out of the traditional order. It's important to validate whatever you are feeling and allow yourself to experience the full range of emotions without judgment. Engaging in self-care activities and seeking support from friends, family, or support groups can also provide comfort and facilitate healing during this challenging time. Remember, grieving the loss of a beloved pet is not a process to be rushed. It is a testament to the depth of the bond you shared, and each step you take towards healing is a step towards honoring that bond.

The Role of Pets in Our Lives: An Emotional Perspective

Emotional Anchors

In the tapestry of life's challenges, pets often serve as steadfast emotional anchors. They provide stability and love, becoming pillars in our lives amidst personal upheavals or external stressors. For anyone who has ever felt the comforting nuzzle of a dog after a harrowing day or heard the soothing purr of a cat during moments of anxiety, the stabilizing presence of pets is undeniable. This anchoring role is particularly significant as it extends beyond mere companionship to encompass a deeper, more therapeutic interaction. Pets often sense our emotional upheaval and respond with acts of affection that provide immediate relief and long-term emotional support. Their ability to remain present with us without judgment or expectation offers a unique form of emotional security. In therapeutic settings, animals are increasingly recognized for their ability to help stabilize emotions. Programs incorporating animals into mental health regimes often report higher levels of success with patients who struggle with depression or PTSD, showcasing the profound impact pets can have as emotional anchors.

Social Catalysts

The role of pets extends outward into the social sphere where they act as catalysts for human interaction. For individuals who might find socializing challenging, pets can bridge gaps, providing common ground with others. Dog parks are quintessential examples where pet owners, who might otherwise never interact, share experiences and conversations, brought together by the communal activity of walking their dogs. Pets often break down barriers of awkwardness and isolation by initiating unplanned interactions such as a horse's neigh or whinny, or through a playful chase, or a rabbit's tumble, purring by a parrot, or an intrigued sniff that leads to a conversation between owners. This aspect is particularly vital in today's world where loneliness is increasingly prevalent. For the elderly or those without immediate family, pets can be a link to the community, often providing reasons for their owners to engage in social activities. Events like pet shows or even casual meet-ups in communal living environments underscore the role pets play in facilitating social connections that are crucial for mental health and emotional well-being.

Routine and Purpose

Caring for a pet instills a sense of routine and purpose that is both grounding and enriching. The responsibilities associated with pet care, feeding, grooming, and exercise demand regularity and commitment, shaping the daily lives of pet owners. This structured routine provides a scaffold for days that might otherwise feel shapeless, particularly during times of personal uncertainty or change. Moreover, the act of caring for another life enhances an individual's sense of self-worth and purpose. For instance, the simple act of feeding a pet provides tangible evidence of one's role in this symbiotic relationship, reinforcing feelings of self-worth through the act of nurturing. This routine and the responsibilities it entails foster a productive environment where both pet and owner benefit, creating a purposeful dynamic that supports mental health and emotional stability.

Unconditional Acceptance

Perhaps one of the most profound aspects of the pet-owner relationship is the unconditional acceptance pets provide. They do not judge by social standards, successes, failures, or appearances; their acceptance is all-encompassing. This unconditional nature offers a safe space for owners to express emotions openly, without fear of judgment or repercussion. In moments of sorrow, a pet's mere presence, free of demands and full of acceptance can be more comforting than the well-meaning words of humans that might sometimes miss the mark. This aspect of pet ownership not only enhances everyday emotional health but also provides significant therapeutic benefits. Individuals recovering from addiction or dealing with mental health issues often report that the nonjudgmental acceptance from their pets is key to their recovery and emotional well-being. Pets provide a constant reminder that they are worthy of love and care, a message that can be life-changing for those who struggle with self-acceptance and self-love.

By fulfilling these roles, pets weave themselves into the fabric of our emotional lives, becoming integral to our well-being. As we continue to understand and appreciate these relationships, it becomes clear that pets do much more than fill our lives with joy and companionship; they touch the very essence of our emotional and social existence, shaping our daily lives in ways both subtle and profound.

Understanding the Psychological Impact of Pet Loss

The psychological impact of losing a pet is profound and multifaceted, touching upon aspects of our identity, our routines, and our emotional landscape. For many pet owners, their pets are not just animals but integral members of their lives, woven into the fabric of their identity. When a pet passes away, it is not uncommon for owners to experience a crisis of self-perception. This can manifest particularly strongly in individuals who define themselves significantly through their relationship with their pets. For instance, someone who is known in their community as the person who always walks their dog in the local park every morning might feel a sense of role loss alongside their grief. This change can trigger a reevaluation of self; who are they without their pet? The void left by a pet's death often extends beyond the absence of physical presence to include a profound impact on the owner's sense of self and purpose.

The sense of loss experienced can be overwhelming, encompassing not only the loss of companionship but also the disruption of daily routines and the physical absence of the pet. This loss is felt in the quiet moments once filled with the sounds of a pet moving through the house, in the spaces where a pet's bed or toys were placed, and in the routines that structured the day around walks, feedings, and playtime. Each of these elements formed part of a shared life, and their absence can leave a palpable emptiness. Adjusting to this new normal often requires reorienting one's day-to-day life, which can be a painful process filled with reminders of the loss.

Additionally, feelings of guilt and regret are common responses following the death of a pet. Owners often ruminate on their pet's final days, questioning their decisions regarding veterinary care or their ability to prevent the death. These feelings can be compounded by the responsibility pet owners often feel for their pet's well-being. To address these painful emotions, it is crucial to engage in self-compassion and to seek reassurance through conversations with veterinarians or fellow pet owners who can provide perspective and validation of the owner's decisions. Understanding that these feelings of guilt are a normal part of the grieving process can also aid in alleviating some of their burdens.

Secondary losses following a pet's death also contribute to the overall grief experience. These may include the loss of a sense of security that the pet provided, changes in social interactions (such as those that occurred during walks or visits to the vet), and the impact on other pets in the household who may also grieve the loss or show signs of stress. Recognizing these secondary losses is important, as they often go unacknowledged, yet they compound the overall experience of grief. Addressing these losses involves creating new routines and finding alternative sources of security and social interaction, which can help in restoring balance and well-being in the owner's life.

Understanding the layers of psychological impact following the loss of a pet illuminates the depth of the bond between humans and their animal companions. It also highlights the necessity for providing support and resources to navigate this difficult time, emphasizing that the grief felt is both real and deserving of recognition. As we continue to explore these themes, the resilience of the human spirit is evident, as is the enduring impact of the love shared with a pet. This love, though it comes with the risk of profound grief, also provides a profound source of comfort and connection that can continue to inspire long after the pet has passed.

Chapter 2: Recognizing and Validating Your Grief

As you find yourself turning the pages of this book, perhaps with a heavy heart and a sense of disbelief that the pet who was once a vibrant presence in your life is no longer by your side, it is essential to acknowledge and validate your feelings. Grief, in its rawest form, can feel like an unwelcome intruder that's messy, overwhelming, and often isolating. However, understanding that these emotions are a normal and valid response to your loss is the first step towards healing. This chapter is dedicated to affirming your grief, offering you the permission to fully experience it, and guiding you towards practices of self-compassion that can provide comfort during this vulnerable time.

It's Okay to Not Be Okay: Validating Your Grief

Normalizing Grief

In a society that often rushes to mask discomfort or rapidly move past sadness, it's important to assert that grief is a natural response to loss; especially a loss as significant as that of a beloved pet. Your pet was not just an animal but a cherished companion, a family member whose unconditional love and presence enriched your life daily. The depth of your sorrow reflects the depth of your bond, and feeling devastated, lost, or even numb are natural emotions that many experience under the weight of such a loss. It's okay to not be okay when you are mourning. By acknowledging your grief, you allow yourself the space to understand and work through your emotions, rather than suppressing them, which is a crucial step in the healing process.

Emotional Spectrum

Grief does not present itself in a uniform way; it encompasses a spectrum of emotions that can vary widely from one person to another. You might find yourself oscillating between sadness and anger, relief and guilt, especially if your pet was suffering before passing away. At times, you might even catch yourself smiling or laughing as you recall fond memories, only to feel sorrow once more. Each of these emotions is a valid response to your loss. It's important to recognize and accept this variability, understanding that grief can manifest in different ways and that each emotion plays a role in your journey towards healing. Allowing yourself to feel these emotions without judgment is a critical part of processing your grief.

Permission to Grieve

Here, you are granted unequivocal permission to grieve. Mourning the loss of your pet is not an overreaction; it is a necessary and healthy response to a significant loss. Take the time you need to grieve, to cry, to remember, and to heal. Set aside moments in your day to reflect on the joy your pet brought into your life and the space they occupied in your heart. Create rituals that help you express your grief, whether it's lighting a candle every evening in their memory, compiling a photo album, or writing down stories about your life together. Engaging in these acts of remembrance can be therapeutic and can serve as a testament to the love you shared.

Self-Compassion

During this intensely vulnerable time, practicing self-compassion is essential. Be gentle with yourself, recognizing that grief can affect your mental, emotional, and physical health. It's okay to reduce your workload, to step back from social obligations, or to simply take a day off when you feel overwhelmed. Treat yourself with the same kindness and understanding that you would offer a good friend in mourning. Consider incorporating practices that nurture your well-being, such as meditation, gentle exercise, or spending time in nature. Each act of self-care is a step towards healing, reinforcing your resilience and ability to cope with the pain of your loss.

When you embrace these principles, you begin to normalize your grief, accept the emotional spectrum of mourning, grant yourself permission to grieve, and practice self-compassion. This will create a foundation for healing that honors both your feelings and the memory of your beloved pet. As you continue to navigate through these pages, remember that this book is a safe space designed to support and guide you through each stage of your grief, helping you to find solace and eventually, a renewed sense of peace.

Common Misconceptions About Pet Loss Grief

In grappling with the loss of a pet, you might encounter widespread misconceptions that can complicate your grieving process. Common sayings like "It's just an animal" or expectations that you should swiftly move past your grief are not only hurtful but profoundly misunderstand the bond shared between you and your pet. These myths need addressing, not just to defend your right to grieve but also to shed light on the truth about mourning a beloved animal companion.

Debunking Myths

The notion that "it's just an animal" seeks to trivialize the relationship you had with your pet. However, as any pet owner knows, the bond with a pet is as meaningful and as rich as any human relationship. Pets are not just animals; they are family members, confidants, and companions in the journey of life. They celebrate with us in moments of joy and comfort us in times of distress, responding to our emotions with an empathy that often surpasses human capabilities.

When someone diminishes their death with "it's just an animal," it overlooks these profound connections. It's essential to confront this myth by sharing about the depth of your relationship, perhaps explaining how your pet was there through significant life changes or how their presence helped you cope with personal challenges. By doing so, you validate the significance of your loss and educate others on the complexity of pet-human relationships.

Another damaging cliché is the expectation to quickly get over the loss. Grief has no timetable, and the healing process differs vastly from one person to another. The idea that you should move on quickly from grieving your pet not only undermines the depth of your bond but also pressures you to suppress your emotions, which can lead to unresolved grief. Counter this myth by allowing yourself the time you need to mourn and by embracing your grief without shame. Sharing your process can help others understand and might encourage them to rethink their expectations about grief.

Societal Expectations

Societal norms often dictate a restrained expression of grief that may not provide enough space for you to mourn adequately. You might feel pressured to appear strong or to return to your routine as if nothing has happened. These expectations can be suffocating when you're dealing with a loss that feels like losing a piece of your heart. To navigate these societal pressures, find safe spaces where your grief is validated. Surround yourself with friends, family, or pet loss support groups who understand the magnitude of your loss and offer the compassion you need. Additionally, setting boundaries around your grieving process can empower you to heal on your terms. You might, for instance, choose to share your feelings only with select people who respect your need to grieve or decide to take time off from social functions to allow yourself space to process your emotions privately.

Comparative Grief

Sometimes, well-meaning individuals might compare the loss of a pet to other types of loss, perhaps implying that it's less significant than losing a human. This comparison can be incredibly painful because it dismisses your grief as lesser or unwarranted. It's important to understand that grief is not a competition. The pain you feel from losing your pet is valid and significant, regardless of how it compares to other losses. Each relationship we forge, whether with humans or pets, is unique, and the grief we feel for each loss is uniquely profound. Embrace your feelings as valid and resist comparisons that seek to quantify your pain. Remember, the depth of your grief is a testament to the depth of your love.

Grief Duration

Finally, dispelling the misconception that grief should be short-lived is crucial. The duration of grief is deeply personal and can be affected by the intensity of your bond, your previous experiences with loss, and your overall emotional and psychological resilience. Some people might find peace within months, while others may take years to find a new normal. Whatever your timeline, it is perfectly normal. Healing is not about adhering to a prescribed schedule but about finding a way to carry your memories forward in a manner that honors your pet and suits your emotional needs. Let yourself grieve for as long or as short as you need to. Embrace practices that bring you solace, be it through creating memorials, writing about your pet, or celebrating their life in meaningful ways. Your journey through grief is yours alone, and honoring your personal timeline is a critical part of the healing process.

How Grief Can Differ: Types of Pet Loss

When a beloved pet departs from our lives, the nature of their leaving significantly shapes our experience of grief. Each scenario, be it sudden or anticipated, carries its own distinct emotional challenges and nuances. For instance, the abrupt loss of a pet often leaves you grappling with shock and a prolonged sense of denial. The world may seem unreal, like a puzzle missing a crucial piece, as you struggle to accept that your pet is truly gone. This denial isn't simply a refusal to accept facts; it's a protective buffer for your heart, giving your emotions time to adjust to the new reality. This phase can be particularly intense for those who experience their pet's death due to an accident or a sudden illness, where the lack of warning adds an additional layer of emotional turmoil. The absence of a chance to say goodbye can lead to unresolved feelings, lingering questions, and what-ifs that haunt your thoughts.

On the other hand, when a pet's passing is anticipated, perhaps due to a chronic illness or old age the grief process can look quite different. Here, you might find yourself in a prolonged state of anticipatory grief where you begin to mourn your pet even while they are still alive. This type of grief can involve its own complex emotions, including fear of the coming loss and the anxiety of watching your pet decline. However, it also provides an opportunity to prepare emotionally and mentally, to cherish the remaining time together, and to say goodbye in ways that sudden loss does not permit. This preparation can lead to a more nuanced acceptance of the pet's passing when it does come, but it can also extend the overall period of mourning as you live through the cycle of hope and despair multiple times.

Euthanasia adds another layer of complexity to the grieving process. Choosing to end a pet's suffering is a profound act of love, yet it can stir intense feelings of guilt and doubt. You might question whether you made the decision too soon or too late, or agonize over whether it was the right decision at all. These feelings can cloud your grief, making it difficult to find peace. It's important during these times to remind yourself of the compassion that guided your decision, to talk through your feelings with supportive friends, family, or professionals who can help you see that choosing a peaceful end for a suffering pet is an act of kindness, even though it comes with such heavy emotional costs.

The pain of losing a pet can also be compounded by the uncertainty of a missing pet. Not knowing the fate of a beloved animal can leave you in a limbo of hope and despair, prolonging the grieving process and complicating your emotional recovery. The lack of closure can lead to prolonged searching, both physically for the missing pet and emotionally for answers, which can prevent you from fully experiencing and processing your grief. The ambiguity surrounding a missing pet can be one of the most challenging scenarios to navigate, as the open-ended nature of the loss offers no clear pathway through the usual stages of grief.

Moreover, the death of a pet often results in secondary losses, which can profoundly deepen and complicate grief. These are the less obvious but significant changes that come with losing a pet, such as the loss of routine that structured your days around walks or feedings, or the loss of companionship that filled your home with energy and affection. Each of these secondary losses can evoke grief in their own right, adding layers to the overall mourning process. They represent the numerous ways in which pets are woven into the fabric of our daily lives, and their absence can leave a vast emptiness that goes beyond missing their physical presence.

There are varied landscapes of grief that come with the different types of pet loss and you must understand that each journey is unique and deeply personal. Whether your grief is sudden or anticipated, compounded by euthanasia, marked by uncertainty, or riddled with secondary losses, each carries its own set of challenges. Acknowledging and understanding these differences can help you find appropriate ways to cope and eventually find a pathway to peace, honoring the unique bond you shared with your pet and the love that will forever remain.

The Impact of Sudden vs. Anticipated Loss of a Pet

When the loss of a beloved pet occurs suddenly, without warning, it can feel as though the ground has shifted beneath you. One moment life is normal, and the next, it's as if a significant part of your world has vanished into thin air. This sudden absence can trigger a profound shock, leaving you grappling with a reality that seems both impossible and unbearable. In instances like these, the initial shock can manifest as a numbness, a protective mechanism that insulates you from the full impact of your grief. This numbness might be punctuated by moments of acute pain, as the reality of the loss intermittently breaks through the protective emotional barrier you've unconsciously erected. Such moments can be deeply disorienting, making the early stages of grief feel like a confusing whirlwind of emotion where disbelief and understanding vie for dominance.

This shock can complicate your grief process significantly, often elongating the stages of denial and anger. It's not uncommon to find yourself revisiting the moment of loss repeatedly, trying to make sense of how something so vital could be so abruptly removed from your life. Questions of "Why?" and "How could this happen?" might dominate your thoughts without providing any solace. The lack of forewarning with sudden loss means you have had no chance to mentally or emotionally prepare for the absence of your pet, which can intensify feelings of unpreparedness and vulnerability. In these moments, it's important to allow yourself to fully experience the shock and the pain, as denying these feelings can delay the healing process. Instead, acknowledging the impact of the shock, perhaps through talking about it with a trusted friend or therapist, can help you begin to process the reality of your loss.

Conversely, when a pet's passing is anticipated, perhaps due to a long illness or simply the culmination of old age, there exists an opportunity for preparation that sudden loss does not afford. This preparation is not just logistical, involving decisions about end-of-life care, but also deeply emotional. You may find yourself beginning the grieving process well before your pet actually passes, mentally and emotionally bracing for the inevitable. This anticipatory grief can help mitigate the shock when the loss finally occurs, but it also introduces its own challenges. You might find yourself constantly on edge, caught between making the most of your remaining time together and the emotional exhaustion of waiting for the loss that you know is coming. This prolonged period of anticipation can lead to fatigue, both emotionally and physically, as the sustained stress takes its toll.

Both sudden and anticipated losses carry with them a burden of guilt and second-guessing. In sudden losses, you might torment yourself with "what if" scenarios such as, what if you had noticed something was wrong sooner, what if you had acted differently, could you have prevented their death? These thoughts can be intrusive and unrelenting, feeding into the anger and denial that complicate early grief. In anticipated losses, while you may have more time to ensure you're providing all possible care, the questions may shift to "did I do enough?" or "did I make their final days comfortable?" You might wonder if there was more that could have been done, or if you made the right decisions regarding their care. This second-guessing can lead to a persistent guilt that overshadows your mourning, making it difficult to focus on the good times you shared instead of the circumstances of their passing.

The timeline for grieving can also vary greatly between sudden and anticipated losses. With sudden loss, the extended period of shock and denial can lead to a longer overall grieving process. You may find yourself feeling fine one day, only to be overwhelmed by grief the next, as the reality of the loss sinks in over time. In contrast, with anticipated loss, while you might begin grieving earlier, the acceptance may come sooner as well, having had time to mentally and emotionally reconcile with the impending loss. However, this is not to say that one type of loss is easier to deal with than the other, each carries its unique set of emotional challenges and requires its own path toward healing.

The aftermath of a pet's death, whether sudden or anticipated, involves acknowledging and respecting the unique challenges each type of loss presents. By understanding these differences, you can better tailor your coping strategies to fit your specific situation, ensuring that you give yourself the best possible support through this difficult time. Remember, there is no right or wrong way to feel after the loss of a pet; there is only your way, and whatever your path, it is valid.

The Importance of Acknowledging Your Pain

In the quiet aftermath of losing a pet, you may find yourself surrounded by well-meaning advice to "stay strong" or to "keep busy," suggestions that might lead you to think that acknowledging your pain is somehow a step backward in your healing. However, the truth is quite the opposite. Recognizing and validating your own feelings of loss is not only a crucial step in your emotional recovery but a necessary one. It's the process of confronting these feelings directly, rather than sidestepping them, that catalyzes true healing.

Acknowledgment as Healing

Understanding that acknowledgment is integral to healing begins with recognizing that grief, although deeply personal, follows certain universal patterns. One of these is that burying or ignoring emotional pain generally prolongs it, allowing it to surface later in more disruptive ways. Conversely, confronting this pain and really sitting with it and understanding its depth, can lead to a more thorough and resilient healing process. Think of it as tending to a wound; it needs to be cleaned and cared for, not ignored, to heal properly. In the context of pet loss, this might mean allowing yourself moments to fully embrace the sadness or the void left by your pet's absence. It could involve looking at their pictures, visiting spots you enjoyed together, or simply sitting with your memories, allowing yourself to feel the loss fully. This active acknowledgment helps to process the emotional reality of your loss, integrating your experiences into your emotional recovery.

Avoidance vs. Confrontation

The effects of avoiding grief versus confronting it can be stark. Avoidance may seem appealing; it is often less painful in the short term and offers a temporary escape from dealing with your emotions. You might throw yourself into work, overbook your social calendar, or take up new hobbies, anything to keep your mind occupied. However, the relief provided is often fleeting, and the unresolved grief can manifest in unexpected ways, such as irritability, sleep disturbances, or even physical symptoms like headaches or fatigue. In contrast, confronting your grief involves facing these uncomfortable emotions head-on. It's about giving yourself permission to grieve and understanding that doing so is a vital part of the healing process. This confrontation helps in accepting the reality of your loss, allowing you to adjust to life without your beloved pet while honoring the relationship you shared.

Finding Support

Surrounding yourself with people who acknowledge and validate your pain is another critical element of healing. Support can come from family, friends, pet loss support groups, or professional counselors. The key is to connect with individuals who understand the significance of your loss and offer the empathy and space you need to grieve. Such environments not only provide comfort but also reinforce the normalcy of your feelings. They can act as a mirror, reflecting your emotions and experiences back to you, which helps in processing grief. If you find yourself in circles where your grief is minimized or misunderstood, it might be necessary to seek out additional or alternative sources of support where your feelings are validated and where you can speak openly about your loss without fear of judgment.

Journaling and Reflection

Incorporating journaling or reflective practices can be particularly effective in acknowledging and processing your grief. Writing about your feelings and experiences can provide a release and serve as a form of therapy. You might write letters to your pet, recounting the memories you cherish or expressing the feelings you weren't able to voice. Alternatively, maintaining a grief journal can provide a structured way to document and explore your emotions on a daily basis. These writings can become a private, sacred space where all your feelings are allowed and acknowledged, a place where your grief is seen and heard, even if only by the pages of your journal. This practice not only helps in processing the emotions at the moment but can also offer insightful reflections on your healing journey over time, showing you how far you've come and the ways in which you've grown and adapted since your loss.

Embracing these practices, acknowledging your pain, confronting your grief directly, seeking supportive environments, and engaging in reflective journaling aren't just steps towards healing; they are affirmations of your love for your pet and the impact they had on your life. They honor your relationship and the bond you shared, ensuring that while your pet may no longer be by your side, the love you have for them continues to be acknowledged and cherished in your journey forward.

Dealing with Dismissive Attitudes Towards Pet Loss

When coping with the loss of a beloved pet, encountering dismissive attitudes from others can add an additional layer of distress to your already heavy heart. It's not uncommon to face comments that undermine the depth of your grief, leaving you feeling misunderstood and isolated. Managing these interactions requires tact and strength, and here, we explore strategies to handle dismissiveness effectively, protect your emotional space, and seek understanding from those around you.

Dismissiveness

The first step in dealing with dismissive attitudes is recognizing that not everyone understands the profound bond shared between a pet and its owner. For some, a pet might simply be an animal, but for you, they were a family member whose loss feels as significant as that of a human loved one. When faced with dismissive remarks, it can be helpful to respond with calm and collected explanations about what your pet meant to you. Explaining the role your pet played in your life can sometimes help others see the emotional impact of your loss. However, it's also important to choose your battles wisely. Some individuals may never truly understand, and recognizing when to disengage can save you from further emotional drain. Instead, focus your energy on maintaining your composure and seeking support from those who do understand and validate your feelings.

Seeking Understanding

Communicating the depth of your grief effectively can sometimes turn dismissive attitudes into empathetic understanding. When sharing your feelings, be as open as you feel comfortable, detailing not just the fact that you are grieving, but how the grief affects you daily. Describe the emptiness in your home without your pet's presence, the silence where there once was the sound of their movements, or how certain routines now bring a sense of loss. These specific details can provide tangible examples of your grief, making it more relatable to others. Additionally, sharing memories of your pet can illustrate the bond you shared, further conveying the significance of your loss. It's also beneficial to express what kind of support you need. Whether it's a listening ear, space to talk about your pet, or simply the acknowledgment of your grief, letting others know how they can help can guide them on how to respond to you during this difficult time.

Protecting Emotional Space

Setting boundaries is crucial in protecting your emotional well-being, especially when dealing with dismissive attitudes. If certain individuals consistently undermine your feelings, it may be necessary to limit your interactions with them, at least temporarily. This doesn't necessarily mean cutting ties, but rather giving yourself permission to excuse yourself from conversations or situations that feel emotionally unsafe. Creating these boundaries allows you to preserve your energy and dedicate it towards healing rather than defending your right to grieve. Remember, it's okay to prioritize your needs and step back from relationships that are not supportive. Additionally, creating a safe emotional space can involve surrounding yourself with reminders of your pet that bring comfort, such as keeping their pictures around or maintaining a small memorial. These acts can serve as affirmations of your right to grieve and celebrate the life of your pet in your own way.

Finding Community

One of the most effective ways to combat dismissive behavior is by connecting with others who understand and share your experiences. Look for pet loss support groups, both in person and online, where you can express your feelings without fear of judgment. These groups provide a platform to share stories and memories of your pets, offering comfort and understanding from those who empathize with your loss.

Additionally, engaging in forums or social media groups dedicated to pet lovers can also provide a sense of community. Here, the shared love for pets fosters a natural empathy for each other's loss, offering a collective shoulder to lean on. Participating in these communities not only helps you feel understood but also provides you with the opportunity to support others in their grief, creating a reciprocal environment of healing and compassion. Through these connections, you reaffirm that you are not alone in your feelings, and that your grief, just like your love for your pet, is real and valid.

When Grief Hits Hard: Identifying Complicated Grief

While many aspects of grief can feel overwhelming, there are specific signs that indicate your experience may be veering into what professionals refer to as complicated grief. This form of grief is characterized by its extended duration and the significant impairment it causes to your life, emotions, and overall functioning. Recognizing the signs of complicated grief is crucial, as it can often require more specialized interventions to navigate successfully. These signs might include persistent sadness that doesn't seem to improve, an inability to think about anything other than your lost pet, feeling that life is meaningless without them, or intense feelings of guilt or anger that don't subside. You might also find yourself withdrawing from social activities you once enjoyed, or feeling like you can't talk about your pet without becoming overwhelmingly emotional.

Understanding when and how to seek professional help is pivotal in cases of complicated grief. While friends and family can offer important support, a mental health professional specializing in grief counseling can provide the tools and techniques to manage your grief more effectively. Finding the right support often starts with speaking to your primary care provider who can refer you to specialists. Additionally, look for counselors or therapists who list grief as an area of focus, or consider support groups specifically for those grieving the loss of pets. These professionals and groups can offer not only understanding and validation but also structured ways to work through your grief.

Triggers for complicated grief can often be subtle and unexpected, making them difficult to manage. Common triggers include anniversaries, seeing your pet's favorite toys, or visiting places you went to together. These moments can suddenly reignite your grief, making you feel as though you've made no progress in your healing. Learning to manage these triggers involves recognizing them in advance where possible and developing coping strategies such as planning ahead on anniversaries or rearranging your home to lessen the impact of seeing your pet's belongings every day. Sometimes, simply being prepared for the possibility of a grief trigger can make them easier to handle.

Despite the challenges of complicated grief, there are countless stories of resilience and recovery that can offer hope. People find strength and healing through support groups, therapy, and sometimes by channeling their experiences into activities that honor their pet's memory, such as volunteering at animal shelters or starting pet-related projects. These actions do not erase the pain, but they can help channel your grief into something that feels meaningful. Over time, with the right support and coping strategies, the sharp edges of grief soften, allowing those affected to remember their pets with more love than pain. This transformation is not quick, but it is a testament to the strength of the human spirit, to endure, adapt, and find ways to carry love forward, even after such a significant loss.

Emotional First Aid: Self-Care in the Wake of Loss

Maneuvering through the aftermath of losing a beloved pet calls for a gentle approach to self-care, which can serve as your emotional first aid. This is not about indulgence but about finding and applying those small, daily measures that can support you through your grief. The connection between taking care of your physical needs and improving your emotional health cannot be overstated, each influences the other significantly. During times of emotional stress, ensuring that your physical health is not neglected is crucial, as the mind and body are deeply interconnected. Engaging in regular, gentle exercise can be a powerful tool in managing stress and improving mood. This isn't about strenuous workouts but rather about activities like walking or light yoga, which help release endorphins and provide a change in scenery, which can shift your perspective momentarily away from your grief.

Furthermore, maintaining or adapting your daily routines provides a framework of normalcy during a time that feels anything but normal. Routines can act as anchors, offering predictability when life seems uncertain. Whether it's your morning coffee, an evening walk, or a nighttime reading ritual, these small acts of normalcy can be profoundly comforting. They remind you that despite the profound loss, the structure of your life remains, offering both comfort and a pathway to gradually rebuild and renew your daily existence without your pet.

Engaging in creative expression offers another therapeutic avenue to explore your feelings and memories related to your pet. Art, whether through painting, writing, or music, allows for a cathartic expression of grief. It provides a physical manifestation of your emotions, which can be particularly healing. You might paint a portrait of your pet, write poems or stories about your experiences together, or compose music that captures the essence of what they meant to you. These creative acts not only help process your emotions but also create lasting tributes to your pet, celebrating their life and the impact they had on you.

By incorporating these self-care strategies into your routine, you not only honor your need to grieve but also reinforce your capacity to cope with and eventually heal from the loss of your beloved companion. Each step, whether a walk in the park, a moment of reflection, or a brushstroke on canvas, is a step toward acknowledging and living with your grief in a way that fosters healing and honors the memory of your pet.

This chapter serves as a reminder of the small yet significant ways you can support yourself through the difficult times following the loss of your pet. From understanding the vital connection between physical activity and emotional health to finding solace in the routines and creative expressions that bring comfort, each strategy is a tool in your emotional toolkit, helping you navigate through your grief with care and compassion. As we move forward, keep in mind these gentle approaches to self-care, carrying with you the knowledge that each day offers new opportunities for healing and remembrance.

Chapter 3: The Grieving Process

S tepping into the immediate aftermath of losing a beloved pet, you may find yourself enveloped in a haze of disbelief and profound silence; a silence that speaks louder than words, echoing the absence of a once vibrant presence in your life. This chapter is dedicated to guiding you through these first disorienting days after your loss, offering a compassionate lens through which to view your reactions, practical advice to manage the immediate necessities, and gentle suggestions for beginning to honor the memory of your cherished companion. Here, you're not alone in your journey through shock and disbelief; instead, you're supported step by step as you manage the phases of grief.

The First Days: Shock and Disbelief

Immediate Reactions

In the initial moments and days following the loss of your pet, you might find yourself caught in a whirlwind of shock and disbelief. This response is a natural protective mechanism, a way for your emotional system to buffer the impact of sudden loss. You might catch yourself expecting to hear their footsteps, see them greeting you at the door, or feel them curling up beside you. These moments, where reality seems to warp, are manifestations of shock; a state where the heart and mind temporarily refuse to accept the finality of what has occurred. It's important to understand and normalize these feelings; they do not signify denial of reality but are part of a natural process of coming to terms with a profound loss. You are not losing your grasp on reality; you are processing deep pain in the only way your mind knows how to handle it at the moment.

Practical Considerations

When the emotional turmoil begins, there are practical matters that require attention, such as caring for your pet's remains. Deciding whether to bury, cremate, or choose another method of burial can be overwhelming. It's helpful to deal with these decisions by considering what would align with the love and care you've always shown your pet. Some find comfort in keeping their pet close by in a custom urn or memorial garden, while others may choose burial in a pet cemetery where they can visit. If making these decisions feels beyond your capacity right now, it's okay to ask for help from family members, friends, or your vet. They can offer support and help handle arrangements according to your wishes and in a way that honors your pet's memory.

Emotional Turmoil

The intense emotional turmoil in the first few days can feel all-consuming. Waves of grief might come with an intensity that takes your breath away, and in these moments, it's crucial to have strategies for self-soothing. Simple acts like deep breathing, listening to calming music, or wrapping yourself in a cozy blanket can provide immediate, albeit temporary, relief. Additionally, don't hesitate to reach out for support. Speaking with friends who understand your bond with your pet, connecting with online support groups, or even seeking the help of a counselor skilled in pet loss grief can offer solace and understanding. These resources can act as a lifeline, reminding you that you are not alone and that your feelings are valid and understood.

Memory and Tribute

Creating a space to remember and honor your pet from the start can be a therapeutic way to begin processing your grief. This might involve setting up a small memorial with their photos, collar, favorite toy, or even lighting a candle daily in their memory. Alternatively, writing a tribute can be a powerful way to articulate your feelings and celebrate the life of your pet. This could be as simple as a letter expressing your love and the things you'll miss, or a more elaborate memoir recounting the joyful times you shared. These acts of remembrance serve as a testament to the bond you shared and can be a profound part of the healing process, anchoring you to the love you have for your pet while handling the pain of their loss.

In embracing these strategies and accepting the tumultuous emotions of the first days, you take essential steps towards acknowledging and honoring both your grief and the life of your beloved pet. Remember that each step, no matter how small, is a part of your path toward healing, and a path towards honoring the connection you shared with your companion.

Anger and Bargaining: Getting Past the Tougher Emotions

When you find yourself grappling with the loss of your beloved pet, it's not uncommon for feelings of anger to surface during the swirl of sorrow and confusion. This anger might catch you off guard; it can be directed at yourself, the circumstances surrounding your pet's passing, or even at others who don't seem to understand the depth of your pain. It's important to recognize that anger is a natural response in the grieving process, often stemming from a sense of injustice or powerlessness. The sudden absence of your pet can leave a palpable void, and anger may arise as a visceral reaction to this abrupt disruption in your life. Understanding that this anger is a normal part of grief can help you accept and process the emotion more healthfully. Instead of suppressing these feelings, acknowledging them as a valid response to your significant loss allows you to begin working through them.

The process of bargaining often accompanies anger. This stage involves the tormenting realm of "what if" and "if only" thoughts that haunt your mind, replaying scenarios where outcomes are different and your pet might still be by your side. Bargaining is a way of negotiating with your pain, an attempt to regain control over something that feels so uncontrollably final. You might find yourself thinking of moments when things could have been done differently, believing that these changes could have spared you and your pet from this ending. It's a painful stage, filled with guilt and regret, but understanding that it is also a normal part of grieving can provide some solace. It's your mind's way of trying to make sense of the loss, to find a reason for the senselessness that often accompanies such profound moments of change.

Finding healthy outlets for expressing and processing both anger and bargaining is crucial. Channeling these emotions into activities such as writing, art, or physical exercise can be incredibly therapeutic. Writing might involve penning letters to your pet expressing the anger and the unanswerable questions, or perhaps journaling about your feelings and the moments you replay in your mind. This can help externalize those thoughts and emotions, making them easier to manage and work through. Artistic expression, whether through painting, sculpture, or music, allows you to encapsulate your emotions in a form that can be both personal and cathartic. Physical activities, particularly those that require focus and exertion, like hiking, running, or yoga, can also provide a healthy outlet for your energy, helping to clear your mind and relieve stress.

Moving beyond these stages of anger and bargaining is pivotal in your path to peace and acceptance. This doesn't mean that the feelings of unfairness or guilt completely vanish, but rather that you start to accept them as part of your grieving process. Integrating these emotions into your understanding of loss allows you to begin moving forward. One strategy for moving beyond anger and bargaining is to consciously shift your focus towards gratitude. Reflecting on the time you had with your pet, the joy and companionship they provided, and the ways they enriched your life can help balance feelings of anger and loss with those of love and gratitude. Engaging in activities that honor their memory, such as creating a memorial space or participating in community events in their name, can also provide a sense of ongoing connection and purpose. These acts of remembrance and celebration help to transform the energy of your grief from something that feels consuming and unbearable into a more gentle and loving tribute to your pet's life.

Moving forward after these complex emotions isn't linear or predictable, but with each small step in expressing, understanding, and integrating these feelings, you make meaningful progress towards healing. Remember, each emotion, no matter how tough, has a role in your larger story of love, loss, and eventual peace.

Depression: Finding Light in the Darkness

Depression is the phase that may feel heavier and more suffocating than those that preceded it. This isn't just sadness or a fleeting mood; it's a more profound, often pervasive feeling of emptiness that can seep into every corner of your life. Recognizing this as a natural part of grieving is crucial, not only for your emotional validation but also for understanding when it might be slipping into something more clinical. Depression in this context can manifest as a loss of interest in activities you once enjoyed, a persistent feeling of sadness that doesn't seem to lift, or a fatigue that rests not just on your body but also on your spirit. You might find yourself withdrawing from social contacts, facing difficulties in maintaining daily routines, or feeling a sense of hopelessness about the future. It's important to delineate these feelings from clinical depression, which is often more enduring and pervasive, potentially hindering your ability to function across different areas of life. If your symptoms persist without relief and start affecting your overall functionality, seeking professional help is a step towards safeguarding your health.

The importance of reaching out for support during this time cannot be overstated. Whether it's professional counseling, connecting with support groups, or leaning on friends and family, each avenue offers unique benefits that can help you navigate through the fog of grief. Professional counselors or therapists specialized in grief can provide tailored strategies that address your specific needs, helping you to understand and process your emotions in a safe and structured environment. Support groups offer the comfort of community; the offer a collective of individuals who have experienced similar losses, where you can share your feelings without fear of judgment and find solidarity in shared experiences. Friends and family can offer a more personal comfort, providing a shoulder to lean on and a willing ear to listen. Each of these supports acts as a beacon, guiding you through the darker days and reminding you that you are not alone in your journey.

The weight of depression, and fostering self-compassion becomes an essential practice. It's about permitting yourself to grieve at your own pace, without rushing the process or berating yourself for not being 'strong enough.' Self-compassion involves recognizing that healing is not linear and that it's okay to have days when you feel you've regressed. Patience with yourself, acknowledging small victories, and setting realistic expectations are all facets of this practice. It's also about treating yourself with the same kindness and understanding that you would offer a good friend in distress. This might mean setting aside periods during the day for rest and reflection, engaging in gentle self-care practices, or simply giving yourself permission to feel whatever emotions arise without judgment.

Finding moments of joy and light might seem like a distant thought when you are in the depths of grief-related depression, but these moments are vital sparks that can gradually illuminate the path to healing. They often lie in simple pleasures and familiar routines. Engaging in activities that connect you with nature, like walks in the park, gardening, or sitting by a lake, can offer a soothing backdrop against which you can feel, heal, and reflect. Nature has a rhythm, a predictability, and a beauty that can be comforting in times of turmoil. Similarly, revisiting hobbies and interests that have brought you joy in the past can also serve as a gentle reminder of the pleasures life holds. Whether it's reading, painting, cooking, or listening to music, allow yourself to reconnect with these activities without any pressure to feel a certain way. These moments of engagement can act as brief respites, helping to lift the heaviness of grief even if just for a short while.

Getting through depression after the loss of a pet is undeniably challenging, but with the right tools and support, it is a landscape you can traverse with hope. Remember, each small step you take towards recognizing your feelings, seeking support, practicing self-compassion, and finding moments of joy is a stride towards regaining your balance and finding light from within the darkness.

Acceptance: Embracing the New Normal

Acceptance in the context of losing a beloved pet does not imply that the pain of loss is over, or that the memories of your pet no longer stir emotions. It signifies a point in your grieving process where the intensity of initial grief transforms into a more reflective and integrative phase. This stage is marked by a gradual understanding and eventual acceptance of the reality that your pet is no longer physically present, yet they continue to live on in your memories and the impact they had on your life. Acceptance allows you to begin looking forward once more, finding ways to adjust to life without your pet while still honoring the significant role they played.

In this phase, creating a legacy for your pet can be a profoundly healing action. This legacy can take many forms, depending on what feels most fitting for the relationship you shared. For some, it involves setting up a scholarship in their pet's name at a local veterinary school, contributing to the future care of animals and the education of those who will care for them. For others, it might mean starting a community project, such as a park cleanup or building a small sanctuary space where people and pets can enjoy time together in a setting that celebrates the bond between humans and animals. Acts of kindness and advocacy carry forward the love and care you had for your pet, transforming grief into proactive, positive outcomes that benefit others.

Adjusting to daily life without your pet involves establishing new routines that no longer include their physical presence but honor the space they occupied in your life. It might start with simple changes, like altering your walking route if your previous one brings back too many painful memories, or repurposing the time you would have spent caring for your pet into volunteering for animal welfare organizations. It could also involve adopting new rituals that help keep your pet's memory alive and part of your everyday life, such as lighting a candle every evening or keeping their favorite toy in a special place. These actions help weave the memory of your pet into the fabric of your daily life, ensuring that their presence is maintained in a new, albeit different, form.

The concept of continued bonds can also be comforting during this stage of acceptance. This psychological model suggests that continuing to foster a connection with a deceased loved one can be a healthy part of grief and adaptation. For pet owners, this might involve talking to your pet as if they were still present, imagining their responses based on the deep understanding you developed over their lifetime. It could also include celebrating their birthdays or adoption days by preparing their favorite treat or sharing stories about them with friends and family. These rituals keep your pet's memory vibrant and integrated into your life, acknowledging that the bond you shared does not simply end with death but transforms into a new form of connection that continues to evolve and provide comfort.

Honoring the Cycle of Grief: Everyone's Timeline is Different

In the delicate aftermath of losing a beloved pet, it's vital to understand that grief does not adhere to a strict schedule or predictable path. Each person's experience of loss is deeply personal, shaped by unique relationships, past experiences, and individual emotional landscapes. This diversity means that there is no universal "right" timeframe for healing. Some may find themselves moving through the stages of grief with a swiftness that surprises them, while others might feel as though their journey through sorrow is a prolonged process, with emotions that linger and resurface even when they think they have moved past them. It's important for you to recognize that both experiences are normal. There's no need to judge yourself harshly if your grief seems to extend longer than others' or if you find yourself revisiting emotions you thought you had overcome. Every journey through grief is unique, and the only correct pace is the one that feels true to your process of healing.

The nature of grief itself is inherently cyclical, not a linear progression from pain to healing. You might find that certain dates, places, or even specific smells can unexpectedly trigger a resurgence of grief, pulling you back into sadness or longing momentarily. This cyclical pattern can be confusing and may feel like a setback in your healing, but it's a normal part of the process. These resurgences are a testament to the depth of your bond with your pet and reflect the profound impact they had on your life. Embracing this cyclical nature of grief helps in understanding that healing is not about reaching a point where you no longer feel the loss, but rather about developing the emotional tools to navigate the waves of sentiment as they come. It's about learning to balance the joy of your memories with the sadness of your loss, allowing each to have its place in your heart.

Respecting your personal grieving process is crucial. It requires honoring your feelings without rush or judgment, allowing yourself the space to mourn in whatever way you need. This might mean setting aside moments in your day for reflection or finding small rituals that help you feel connected to your pet. It also means being patient with yourself when emotions surface unexpectedly and understanding that these moments are part of the rich tapestry of love and memory that you shared with your pet. Giving yourself permission to feel and heal in your time helps in fostering resilience, as it acknowledges the complexity of your emotions and the reality of your loss.

Over time, developing long-term coping strategies becomes essential in integrating the loss of your pet into your life's narrative. This might involve creating lasting memorials or traditions that honor your pet, such as planting a garden or commissioning artwork that reminds you of them. It can also involve more introspective practices, such as writing or meditation, where you can explore and express your feelings in a supportive environment. These activities do more than just serve as outlets for your grief; they help weave the memory of your pet into the ongoing story of your life, allowing you to carry forward their legacy in meaningful ways. Moreover, these practices can evolve and change as you do, adapting to your needs and circumstances as your relationship with your grief shifts over time. As you continue to grow and heal, these strategies can help ensure that your memories of your pet, while tinged with sadness, are also filled with warmth and love, reflecting the complex, beautiful bond you shared.

Finding Closure: Is It Really Possible?

In the quiet aftermath of losing a pet, the concept of 'closure' often surfaces, a term frequently touted as the ultimate end-goal of grieving. Yet, the traditional notion of closure, where emotions are neatly resolved and the book of grief is closed, may not resonate with everyone's experience. Rather than viewing closure as a definitive end point, it's often more helpful to consider it as achieving a state of peace or coming to terms with the loss. This perspective acknowledges that while the sharp pain of grief may ease, the memories and impact of a beloved pet can continue to influence your life positively.

The theory of Continuing Bonds offers a refreshing viewpoint on this ongoing connection. This approach suggests that maintaining a continuing relationship with your deceased pet through memories and rituals can be a healthy part of grieving. It contrasts sharply with older models of grief, which advocated for detachment and moving on as markers of successful grieving. Instead, Continuing Bonds embraces the idea that keeping your pet's memory alive, talking about them, imagining them in daily life, or even setting places for them during special occasions can be comforting. This ongoing internal relationship can help integrate the loss into your life, allowing you to carry forward the love and lessons learned from your pet.

Creating a lasting memorial can also serve as a form of closure that doesn't signify forgetting but rather honoring and remembering. This could be as tangible as planting a tree in your pet's favorite spot in the garden, or as personal as compiling a photo album or a scrapbook filled with memories of times spent together. Each act of memorializing serves as a bridge between your past with your pet and your future without their physical presence, allowing you to revisit memories with a sense of peace rather than raw grief. These tributes stand as testaments to the love shared and the impact your pet had on your life, offering solace and a physical locus for remembering.

Accepting that grief can be an ongoing journey marks a significant shift in understanding. It allows for a more flexible, realistic view of emotional healing. Grief might lessen in intensity over time but expecting it to disappear entirely might set you up for frustration. Instead, acknowledging that moments of sadness, longing, or remembrance might surface periodically, especially during milestones or certain times of the year, can prepare you to handle them with grace. These moments are not setbacks but are part of a landscape of healing where memories of your pet continue to play a meaningful role in your life.

As this chapter closes, the key points to embrace are the redefinition of closure, the therapeutic potential of maintaining ongoing bonds, the comforting role of memorials, and the acceptance of grief as a continuing journey. Each element contributes to a broader understanding of grief, one that accommodates a range of experiences and emotions. As you move forward, remember that the path of grief is deeply personal, and finding peace is a gradual process enriched by the memories and ongoing presence of your beloved pet in your life.

Moving into the next chapter, we will explore how community and shared experiences can further support and enrich your journey through pet loss, providing new perspectives and compassionate understanding from others who have walked similar paths.

Chapter 4:
Practical Coping
Strategies

I n the stillness that follows the storm of emotions brought on
by the loss of a beloved pet, finding a path forward can seem
daunting. You may feel adrift, uncertain of how to begin managing
your grief. Practical coping strategies, particularly those that involve
creating rituals and memorials, offer a tangible way to honor your
pet's memory while providing a structured means of processing your
emotions. This chapter focuses on harnessing the healing power of
rituals and memorials, guiding you through the thoughtful creation
of ceremonies and physical tributes that reflect the unique bond you
shared with your pet. These acts of remembrance not only serve as a
comfort during times of sorrow but also as a celebration of the life and
love you and your pet shared.

Harnessing the Power of Rituals and Memorials

Creating Meaningful Rituals

The creation of personalized rituals can be a profound way to channel your grief into actions that honor your pet's memory. These rituals can vary widely, from simple daily gestures to more elaborate ceremonies, depending on what resonates most with you. A morning ritual might involve spending a few moments at your pet's favorite spot in the garden, perhaps sharing your thoughts or reading aloud as if they were still by your side.

For more formal rituals, consider an annual remembrance ceremony on the anniversary of your pet's passing, inviting friends and family to share stories and celebrate the joy your pet brought into your lives. The key to these rituals is their personal significance; they should reflect your relationship and the things that were special about your pet. For instance, if your dog loved the beach, a yearly gathering by the shore to toss flowers into the surf could be a beautiful way to remember them. These rituals help weave the memory of your pet into the fabric of your daily life, allowing you to honor their legacy in a way that feels active and ongoing.

Designing a Memorial Service

If you choose to hold a memorial service, planning one that captures the essence of your pet's personality and the bond you shared can be a cathartic part of your grieving process. Start by selecting a location that holds special meaning such as, a favorite park or even your backyard. Consider the elements of the service, such as readings, music, or eulogies, that might best reflect your pet's spirit. For a cat who loved lounging in the sun, a reading about the joy of simple pleasures might be fitting, or for a lively dog, an upbeat song that recalls their zest for life. Encourage attendees to share their memories, creating a tapestry of tales that celebrate your pet's life from multiple perspectives. This gathering not only serves as a tribute but also as a communal healing experience, allowing those who knew your pet to find comfort in shared memories and collective mourning.

The Role of Memorials

Physical memorials serve as enduring tributes to your pet, providing a tangible focus for your memories and a place to connect with the emotions of loss and love. Planting a tree in their honor, for instance, offers a living memorial that grows and changes with the seasons, symbolizing the ongoing nature of your love. Alternatively, creating a garden stone with your pet's name or a simple plaque can act as a reminder of their presence in your life. These memorials can be placed in a garden, along a favorite walking path, or in any space that was significant to you and your pet. They serve as sacred spaces where you can go to remember, to reflect, or simply to feel closer to your pet, providing a physical embodiment of the memories that you carry in your heart.

Community Involvement

Involving friends, family, and others who knew your pet in the creation of memorials or in memorial services can amplify the healing power of these rituals. It allows those who shared in your pet's life to contribute their own memories and support, weaving a communal tapestry of remembrance that underscores the impact your pet had on the lives of others. Whether it's helping to plant a memorial garden or sharing stories during a service, this collective involvement creates a support network that reinforces the significance of your loss while also celebrating the joy your pet brought to multiple lives. It is a reminder that while your grief is deeply personal, you are not alone in your memories or your mourning.

By embracing these strategies, you create not only a legacy of love and memory for your pet but also a framework for your own healing journey. These rituals and memorials offer ways to channel your grief into actions that honor your pet's life, providing comfort and connection during your time of loss. Through these acts of remembrance, you continue to celebrate the bond you shared, finding solace in the knowledge that love, once given, remains a part of us; forever remembered, forever cherished.

Creative Expression: Journaling, Art, and More

Journaling for Emotional Release

As you navigate the waves of grief that come with the loss of your pet, finding a safe outlet for your emotions is crucial. Journaling stands out as a powerful tool for emotional release, allowing you to pour out your feelings in a private, unfiltered way. Think of a journal as a dedicated space where anything goes. Every thought, memory, and emotion you have about your pet can be expressed here without fear of judgment. To start, you might choose a notebook that feels special or comforting to you, perhaps one with a design that reminds you of your pet. In terms of what to write, the possibilities are vast. You might start with the basics of your day, how you felt when you woke up, or what moments triggered memories of your pet. For a more structured approach, consider prompts such as, "Today, I miss...", "I remember when...", or "I feel lost because...". These starters can help you tap into your feelings and may lead to deeper reflections and insights. Over time, your journal can become a cherished repository of memories and a testament to your healing process, providing not only an outlet for your grief but also a record of your journey through it.

Art as Healing

The transformative power of art offers another profound avenue for expressing grief and remembering your beloved pet. Whether you choose painting, sculpture, or digital art, each medium allows you to encapsulate your emotions and memories in a form that resonates with your personal experience and aesthetic sense. If painting, you might use colors that convey the mood of a particular memory or moment shared with your pet. Sculpture could involve creating a piece that symbolizes your relationship or an aspect of your pet's personality that you cherished. Digital art offers the flexibility of combining images, text, and colors to create a vibrant collage of your memories. Engaging in these artistic endeavors allows you to process your feelings in a tangible way, creating artworks that serve as both a tribute to your pet and a form of emotional catharsis. Moreover, the act of creating can be meditative, providing a focus that helps still the chaos of grief, giving you a sense of peace and accomplishment amidst the turmoil of loss.

Music and Healing

Music's capacity to evoke emotions and memories makes it a uniquely effective tool for healing. Creating or compiling playlists that remind you of your pet can be a comforting way to feel connected to them. Consider songs that you used to enjoy together, or tracks that remind you of specific moments or periods in your pet's life. Alternatively, you might create a playlist of calming or soothing music to listen to during moments when your grief feels overwhelming. Music can also be incorporated into memorial services or personal rituals, playing songs that capture the essence of your relationship with your pet. Whether actively creating music or curating playlists, the act of interacting with music provides a therapeutic outlet for your emotions, helping to soothe your spirit and keep your pet's memory alive in a melodious form.

Crafting and DIY Projects

For those who find comfort in tangible activities, engaging in crafting or DIY projects can be a therapeutic way to channel grief into creativity. Scrapbooking is a particularly poignant way to preserve memories, allowing you to compile photos, mementos, and notes that reflect your journey with your pet. Each page can be a dedicated story or theme, decorated with colors, stickers, and tokens that bring the memories to life. Quilting or sewing projects, such as creating a pillow or a blanket from your pet's old beds, toys, or clothing, can transform cherished belongings into comforting keepsakes. Similarly, assembling a photo album or creating a memory box are projects that not only help organize memories but also provide a physical space of remembrance. These crafting activities not only help distract the mind from the pain of loss but also create enduring symbols of love and memory, each stitch, paste, or placement a testament to the enduring bond you shared with your pet.

The Role of Support Groups in Healing

After losing a beloved pet, the support of those who understand your loss can be invaluable. Finding the right support group can offer not only solace but also a sense of community that helps mitigate the loneliness that often accompanies grief. Whether online or in-person, each type of group has its benefits and considerations. Online groups provide accessibility and anonymity, allowing you to connect with support at any time from the comfort of your home, which can be particularly appealing if you find leaving the house difficult during your period of mourning. These forums often host a diverse range of experiences and advice, offering a wide spectrum of support. On the other hand, in-person groups offer a tangible sense of connection and immediacy in interactions, which can be very comforting. The physical presence of others who empathize with your loss can make the support feel more immediate and personal.

When choosing a support group, consider the structure and the facilitation of the group. Groups led by professionals such as grief counselors or veterinarians often provide a structured approach to dealing with grief. These facilitators are trained to guide discussions in a way that is constructive and respectful, ensuring that all members feel heard and supported. They can also offer expert insights into the grieving process, helping you understand and navigate your emotions more effectively. Additionally, these leaders can help maintain the focus of the group, steering conversations away from potentially triggering topics and ensuring the environment remains supportive and beneficial to all members.

Sharing your story in a support group, listening to others' experiences, and realizing you are not alone in your feelings can be incredibly healing. It's often in these shared narratives that you find tips on coping strategies that worked for others, insights into the grieving process, and sometimes, lasting friendships with individuals who understand exactly what you are going through. The communal aspect of these groups reinforces the understanding that grief is a universal emotion, though experienced individually, and that support is available, often making the burden of grief feel lighter as it is shared among peers.

If you find that available groups do not meet your needs or if you're looking for a more specific type of support, consider starting your own group. This can be a rewarding way to give back and find purpose in the wake of your loss, while also tailoring the support to meet specific needs that might not be addressed in other groups. Begin by identifying the focus of the group, whether it's for a particular type of pet, method of loss, or demographic of pet owners. Reach out through local veterinarians, pet stores, or online platforms to find members. Setting clear norms and goals for the group from the outset can help ensure that the group provides a supportive and respectful space for all members. Decide whether you want to lead the group yourself or co-facilitate with another member or professional. As your group grows, the collective wisdom and support can become a powerful tool in helping each member navigate their grief journey.

Engaging in support groups, whether as a member or leader, provides a unique opportunity to connect with others who can empathize with your loss deeply and personally. This connection becomes a bridge over the turbulent waters of grief, offering you and others a passage toward healing, understanding, and eventually, peace.

Physical Wellness - A Path to Emotional Healing

Beware of the emotional turbulence of losing a beloved pet, it's easy to overlook the profound connection between our physical health and our emotional well-being. During such times, engaging in physical activity can serve as a crucial emotional outlet, offering a respite from the cycles of grief. Physical exercise, from brisk walking to more organized sports, stimulates the production of endorphins, the brain's feel-good neurotransmitters. This natural mood lift is a welcome relief when you are grappling with sadness and loss. Moreover, the rhythm and routine of physical activity provide a structure that can seem soothing when much of life feels unpredictable and chaotic. Whether it's a daily jog that clears your mind or a yoga session that helps you feel centered, the simple act of moving your body can help mitigate the intensity of grief, providing not just distraction but a proactive way to cultivate your mental health. Regular exercise also helps improve sleep patterns and reduce anxiety, which are often disrupted by the stress of bereavement. The key is to choose activities that you enjoy and that feel rejuvenating rather than obligatory, allowing the exercise to be a source of comfort and strength during your healing process.

The healing effects of spending time in nature cannot be overstated, especially when coping with emotional pain. Nature, with its inherent beauty and tranquility, offers a unique environment for solace and reflection. Activities like walking through a park, hiking along a trail, or simply sitting beside a lake allow for a communion with the natural world that can be deeply comforting. These moments spent under the open sky, surrounded by the sights and sounds of nature, provide a perspective that can be both grounding and uplifting. The vastness of nature can make personal grief feel a bit smaller, more manageable, and part of a larger cycle of life and renewal. Additionally, being in nature not only reduces feelings of stress and anger but also enhances physical well-being, reducing blood pressure and muscle tension. This synergy of physical and emotional relief makes spending time out-doors a vital component of the healing process. Whether it's a quiet moment listening to the rustle of leaves or a vigorous hike up a hill, each step in nature is a step toward regaining your emotional equilib-rium.

Maintaining balanced nutrition during times of grief is another fun-damental aspect of supporting your overall well-being. Grief can dis-rupt normal eating patterns, leading to undereating, overeating, or an indifference to food. However, the foods you consume play a critical role in how you feel both physically and emotionally. Nutrient-rich foods can boost brain function and enhance mood, while a poor diet can exacerbate feelings of lethargy and depression. It's important to try and maintain a balanced diet, rich in fruits, vegetables, lean proteins, and whole grains, which can help stabilize your mood and energy levels. Hydration is equally crucial, as dehydration can cause or worsen symptoms of fatigue and irritability. If you find it difficult to prepare meals, consider simple yet nutritious options like smoothies or salads that require minimal preparation time. Alternatively, you might cook large meals when you are up to it and freeze portions for days when cooking feels too daunting. Remember, taking care of your body by providing it with nourishing foods is a form of self-care that supports emotional recovery.

Incorporating restorative practices such as yoga, meditation, or tai chi can also play a significant role in managing grief-related stress and promoting inner peace. These practices focus on the connection be-tween mind, body, and breath, helping to alleviate tension and anxiety.

Yoga, for example, combines physical postures with breathing exercises and meditation, making it an excellent tool for reducing emotional stress and improving physical health. Meditation offers a way to quiet the mind, providing a break from the constant cycle of grief-related thoughts. Even a few minutes of meditation can make a significant difference in how you feel, helping to restore a sense of calm and control. Tai chi, often described as meditation in motion, is another gentle way to help keep the body moving and focused while fostering a state of relaxation and balance. Engaging regularly in these practices can provide a valuable emotional outlet and a sense of serene stability during the turmoil of loss, guiding you gently towards a place of peace and acceptance.

Seeking Professional Help: When and How

When the deep waters of grief surface after the loss of a beloved pet, there comes a point where you might feel that your usual coping mechanisms are not enough, and the weight of your sorrow seems too heavy to bear alone. Recognizing when it's time to seek professional help is a crucial step, not only in managing your grief but also in ensuring your overall well-being during this challenging time. It's important to be aware of the signs that indicate your grief has transitioned into a more complex form, potentially hindering your daily functioning and quality of life. These signs might include persistent sadness or depression that doesn't seem to improve over time, intrusive thoughts about your pet's death that prevent you from focusing on other aspects of your life, or feelings of guilt or worthlessness that are difficult to shake. If your grief feels like a constant shadow that colors every part of your day, or if you find yourself withdrawing from relationships and activities that you once enjoyed, these could be indicators that professional help could be beneficial.

Finding a therapist who specializes in grief or pet loss can provide you with the support and guidance necessary to navigate your emotions more effectively. When looking for the right therapist, it's helpful to start by seeking recommendations from your primary care provider or from friends who have had positive experiences with therapy. Many therapists list their specialties on their websites or online profiles, making it easier to find someone with expertise in grief counseling. It's important to consider the therapist's approach and ensure it aligns with your needs; some therapists might use cognitive-behavioral techniques to help you manage intrusive thoughts, while others might focus on providing a space for you to express and process your emotions freely. Don't hesitate to reach out to potential therapists for a preliminary conversation to gauge your comfort level with them and to ask about their experience with pet loss specifically. This initial contact can provide insight into whether their approach and demeanor are a good fit for you.

Therapeutic Modalities

Exploring different therapeutic modalities can also enhance your understanding of what might work best for you in managing your grief. Cognitive-behavioral therapy (CBT) is a widely used approach that focuses on identifying and changing negative thought patterns that can contribute to emotional distress. For someone grieving a pet, CBT can be helpful in addressing feelings of guilt or regret by reshaping how you perceive the events surrounding your pet's death. Art therapy offers a different approach, utilizing creative expression as a means to explore and convey your feelings. This can be particularly beneficial if you find verbal expression challenging or if you connect deeply with visual or tactile forms of communication. Group therapy is another option that brings individuals together who are experiencing similar types of grief, providing a collective environment where you can share experiences and support each other under the guidance of a professional facilitator.

Insurance and Accessibility

Obtaining insurance and accessibility when seeking therapy can sometimes feel daunting, but understanding your options can make this process smoother. Many insurance plans offer coverage for mental health services, so reviewing your policy details or contacting your insurance provider can help you understand what types of therapy and which therapists are covered under your plan. If insurance coverage is not available or if costs are prohibitive, consider looking for therapists who offer sliding scale fees based on your income, making therapy more accessible. Additionally, many therapists now offer online sessions, which can be a convenient option if you have transportation challenges or if you prefer the comfort of receiving therapy in your own home. These online platforms often provide the same level of professional support but with greater flexibility and sometimes at a lower cost.

Recognizing the need for help, finding the right therapist, and exploring various therapeutic modalities, are important steps towards taking care of yourself during a profoundly difficult time. Each step forward is a move towards healing, honoring your bond with your pet while ensuring your own emotional and psychological well-being. As you consider these options, remember that seeking help is a sign of strength and a proactive step in caring for yourself, just as you cared for your beloved pet.

The Healing Power of Nature: Walks, Gardens, and Outdoor Memorials

The solace that nature offers can be profoundly therapeutic, especially when coping with the loss of a beloved pet. Integrating nature into your healing process not only provides a serene backdrop for reflection but also helps maintain a connection with the essence of your pet, who likely enjoyed their own moments under the sky. Regular walks in natural settings, for instance, can become meditative rituals in themselves. These walks allow you to step away from the routine of daily life and immerse yourself in the calming effects of the natural world. Whether it's a quiet path through a local park or a more rugged trail in the wilderness, each step offers a moment to reflect on your memories and the time spent with your pet. The rhythm of walking, coupled with the sensory experience of nature, the sound of leaves rustling, the sight of birds soaring, or the smell of earth after rain can be incredibly grounding, bringing a sense of peace and continuity when you are overcome by the pain of loss.

Creating a memorial garden is another meaningful way to channel your grief into a nurturing project that honors your pet's memory. This garden can be a dedicated space where you plant flowers, shrubs, or even a tree that reminds you of your pet or symbolizes their spirit. For a pet who loved to bask in the sun, sun-loving plants like lavender or sunflowers might be appropriate. Alternatively, a peaceful shade garden can be fitting for a pet who enjoyed lounging in cool, quiet spots. As you design and tend to the garden, each choice and action can be infused with personal significance, turning the act of gardening into a living tribute. Over time, the garden will grow and evolve, offering a living metaphor for the healing process and reminding you that with care and time, new growth and beauty can emerge from grief.

Exploring different types of outdoor memorials can also provide lasting ways to remember your pet. These memorials can range from bench plaques in public parks where you might have enjoyed walks together, to dedicated trees in community gardens or even custom-made statues. Each of these memorials serves not only as a tribute to your pet but also as a permanent marker of their life and the joy they brought into yours. They create a physical space where memories can be revisited and shared with others who might stop to read a plaque or admire a beautifully crafted piece of art. These memorials can become places of reflection and connection, not just for you but for the broader community, enhancing the communal space with stories of love and companionship.

Lastly, engaging in activities such as bird watching or gardening can provide not only a distraction from grief but also a new avenue for joy and fulfillment. Bird watching, for instance, requires patience and quiet, helping to soothe a restless mind and bring one's attention to the beauty of the present moment. Gardening, whether in a personal memorial garden or in community plots, offers a sense of purpose and achievement, as well as the physical benefits of tending to plants. Both activities draw on the healing aspects of nature, allowing for moments of peace and a renewed appreciation for the cycles of life and growth.

Walks for reflection, creating a memorial garden, establishing outdoor memorials, and engaging with nature through bird watching or gardening provide pathways to healing that is enriched by the natural world. They offer opportunities to remember and honor your pet in a setting that speaks to the beauty and continuity of life, helping you navigate your grief with a sense of peace and hope for renewal.

Chapter 4 Conclusion

In this chapter, we explored the therapeutic power of nature and its role in the healing process after the loss of a pet. From the reflective solitude of walks and the creative expression of designing memorial gardens to the establishment of lasting outdoor memorials, each element offers a unique way to cope with grief while honoring the memory of a beloved companion. These activities not only provide comfort but also foster a connection with the natural world, reminding us of the enduring cycle of life and growth. As we turn to the next chapter, we will continue to explore additional strategies that support healing and remembrance, each step guided by the love and memories we hold for our pets.

Chapter 5: Supporting Others in Grief

As the quiet settles after the storm of losing a beloved companion, your own heart will begin to find a rhythm in the new normal. However, you may discover that others, particularly young children, may be struggling with their own choppy waters of grief. Supporting others through their loss, especially children, requires a gentle touch, a patient ear, and a heart ready to understand grief from their perspective. In this chapter, we explore how to help the younger members of your family understand and express their sorrow, ensuring they receive the support they need during such a vulnerable time.

Talking to Children About Pet Loss: A Gentle Approach

Age-Appropriate Explanations

When explaining the loss of a pet to children, it's imperative to tailor your approach to their level of understanding, ensuring the explanation is both honest and sensitive to their developmental stage. Young children often have a limited understanding of death, viewing it as temporary or reversible, a concept similar to characters in cartoons waking up after a fall. Explaining death as a natural, permanent part of life is crucial, yet it should be done with care to avoid causing unnecessary fear. Using simple, clear language, you might say, "Remember how [Pet's name] was very old/sick? Last night, they died. This means that their body stopped working, and they won't be coming back. But we can keep them in our hearts through our memories." This explanation focuses on the pet not suffering anymore and emphasizes the continuity of memory, which can be comforting to a child.

Encouraging Expression

Children, much like adults, need to express their grief, but they might not always have the words to do so. Encouraging them to express their feelings about their lost pet can take various forms, depending on the child's age and interests. Drawing, writing stories, or playing can all be therapeutic. For instance, providing art supplies and suggesting they draw a picture of their favorite memory with their pet allows them to process their feelings through creativity. For older children, writing a letter to their pet expressing their feelings or penning a story about their adventures together can be a meaningful way to cope. These activities provide a physical outlet for their emotions and can help children make sense of their loss.

Rituals for Children

Involving children in rituals or creating new ones can help them say goodbye and begin to heal. A simple, child-friendly ritual might involve lighting a candle daily, allowing them to say a few words about their pet, or even just sitting silently for a few moments. Another idea could be creating a memory box where they can keep photos, toys, or other mementos of their pet. These rituals provide a structure within which children can express their emotions and come to terms with their loss, offering a sense of continuity and security at a time when they might feel particularly vulnerable.

Supporting Through Change

The loss of a family pet can disrupt a child's sense of stability, making the maintenance of daily routines crucial. Keeping meal, bedtime, and other daily routines as consistent as possible can provide a sense of normalcy. It's also important to offer extra reassurance during this time, as children may feel more anxious or insecure about other changes happening around them. Reaffirming your presence and availability, letting them know that it's okay to ask questions or express their feelings anytime, helps them feel supported and understood. This consistent support helps mitigate the fear of further loss, gradually rebuilding their sense of security and normalcy after the upheaval caused by their pet's death.

In guiding children through the grief of losing a pet, the compassion, patience, and understanding you demonstrate not only help them heal but also teach them how to cope with other challenges they will inevitably face in life. Through these discussions, expressions, and rituals, children learn that grief, while deeply painful, is a normal response to loss and that they are supported through their sadness. This foundation of understanding and openness around the topic of loss and grief is a profound gift that helps them grow into empathetic adults, aware of their emotions and capable of supporting others in their times of need. As you navigate this delicate process, remember that your role is to guide and support, allowing the child to lead the way in their grieving process, ensuring it is a journey that acknowledges their feelings and aids in their emotional growth.

Supporting a Partner or Spouse Through Pet Loss

When you and your partner face the loss of a beloved pet, the waves of grief can wash over each of you differently, sometimes pulling you together in shared sorrow, other times isolating you in unique, personal experiences of loss. Recognizing and respecting these differences in grieving is crucial as you navigate this challenging time together. It's important to understand that there is no right or wrong way to feel after the loss of a pet, and what provides comfort to one person may not be the same for another. Your partner might find solace in talking about the pet, reminiscing about the joy brought into your lives, while you might prefer quiet reflection. Open communication becomes your strongest ally here. Encourage discussions about your feelings and needs, and be prepared to listen without judgment or interruption. This kind of dialogue can help you understand where your partner is in their grieving process and show them that they are not alone in their feelings. It also opens up space for expressing what you both might need from each other during this time, whether it's more personal space or more shared activities to honor the memory of your pet.

Creating a shared space for remembering and celebrating your pet can be a beautiful way to bridge individual grieving processes and foster a sense of mutual support and understanding. One way to do this is by compiling a photo album together. This activity allows both of you to revisit cherished memories, each photo a story, a shared smile, or a tear. As you organize the album, encourage each other to share stories or moments associated with each picture. This can be a powerful way to relive the happy moments you spent with your pet and reinforce the joy that your pet brought to your lives. Additionally, consider setting up a small dedicated space in your home with your pet's pictures, their favorite toys, or even a candle. This shared shrine not only honors your pet but also creates a physical space and memorial to facilitate a lasting connection with your pet and to each other.

Providing emotional support to a grieving partner involves a delicate balance of presence and patience. It's about being there, truly listening, and acknowledging their pain without trying to fix it. Active listening is the key to understanding, without response. Let your partner express their feelings without fear of judgment. Acknowledge their pain with responses that affirm their feelings, such as "It's understandable to feel that way," or "I'm really sorry we're going through this." Avoid platitudes like "They're in a better place now," which can sometimes invalidate the very real pain of loss. Instead, focus on empathetic responses that validate their feelings and encourage further sharing. It's also helpful to recognize when to offer distractions or activities, such as taking a walk or watching a favorite movie together, which can provide a temporary respite from grief.

Supporting each other's self-care is another vital aspect of managing pet loss together. It's easy to neglect personal well-being during times of grief, but maintaining physical and emotional health is crucial for both personal and mutual resilience. Encourage each other to engage in self-care activities, whether it's pursuing a hobby, exercising, or simply taking time for rest and reflection. Be proactive in supporting each other's health by planning nutritious meals together or reminding each other to stay hydrated and rested. Remember, taking care of your own well-being enables you to be a better support to your partner. Additionally, consider attending a support group for pet loss together, or seek counseling if the grief feels overwhelming. These resources can provide both individual and joint support, offering strategies to manage grief and helping to strengthen your relationship during this difficult time.

Sharing your feelings with your partner or spouse can deepen your understanding of each other's emotional landscapes and enhance your capacity to support each other through life's challenges. By fostering open communication, creating shared spaces for remembrance, offering empathetic support, and prioritizing mutual self-care, you build a stronger, more resilient bond that honors the love you shared with your pet and with each other.

Helping Friends Grieve and Honor Their Pets

When a friend experiences the loss of a pet, the depth of their grief can be profound and palpable, echoing the loss of a cherished family member. In these moments, the support they receive from friends like you can become a cornerstone of their healing process. Offering practical support starts with understanding the immediate needs your friend might face in the wake of their pet's passing. This could range from helping with the logistics of vet appointments or cremation services to managing the more mundane but overwhelming tasks like household chores or preparing meals. Simply being present, whether for a phone call to share memories or a quiet evening together, can provide an immeasurable comfort. Sometimes, just sitting with your friend, acknowledging their pain without the pressure to fill the silence, can be the most powerful support you offer.

Taking a step further, contributing to a memorial fund or making a donation to an animal charity in the name of your friend's pet can also be a touching gesture that honors the life of the pet while supporting a cause that aids other animals. Such actions not only show deep respect for the bond your friend shared with their pet but also help to create a legacy that extends beyond their grief. These contributions can be accompanied by a sympathy card or a thoughtful note, expressing your understanding and solidarity in their time of loss. It's these thoughtful gestures that often resonate deeply, providing a tangible testament to the life and love shared between your friend and their pet.

Staying connected with your friend in the weeks and months following their loss is crucial. It's important to remember that grief does not have a set timeline and can ebb and flow unpredictably. Sending a text, making a call, or scheduling visits can keep you attuned to their healing process, allowing you to offer support as needed. These check-ins are vital not just for providing company but also for observing any signs that your friend might be struggling to cope, potentially needing more structured support or even professional help. It's during these ongoing conversations and visits that you can gently remind your friend of the care and support available to them, reinforcing that they are not alone in gaining control over their grief.

Sharing in the remembrance of your friend's pet offers another layer of support, helping to celebrate the pet's life and the joy they brought.

If a memorial service is planned, attending and even participating, if appropriate, can be profoundly supportive. Sharing memories or photos during the service, or simply being there to listen to others' stories, can help your friend feel a communal support that might ease the sharpness of their grief. For friends who might not organize formal services, creating informal opportunities to reminisce about the pet, like a small gathering at a favorite park or compiling a photo book of happy memories, can be equally comforting. These acts of shared remembrance not only honor the pet but also strengthen the bond between you and your friend, woven together by shared memories and mutual support during times of loss.

From practical help in the immediate days following the loss to on-going emotional support and shared remembrance, your role as a friend is pivotal. You provide a network of care that helps your friend not only mourn their loss but also celebrate the life of their beloved pet, making the journey through grief a little less lonely. Through thoughtful gestures, consistent presence, and shared memories, you help weave a tapestry of support that honors a cherished pet's memory and shows profound respect for your friend's loss.

Community Memorials and Shared Healing Practices

In the wake of a pet's passing, the collective heart of a community often seeks expression, looking for ways to memorialize and share the burden of grief. Community memorial events stand as a poignant testament to this need, providing a structured space where individuals can come together to remember and celebrate the lives of pets they have loved and lost. These events can vary widely in their format, rang-ing from formal ceremonies at local parks or pet cemeteries to more casual gatherings in community centers or even private homes. The key component is the communal aspect of people coming together, drawn by shared experiences of love and loss, supporting one another in their grief. For instance, organizing a communal event where people can bring photos or items that belonged to their pets, share stories, or even participate in a collective release of biodegradable balloons or lanterns can be incredibly moving. Such events not only provide a sense of closure for those grieving but also reinforce the bonds within the community, making it stronger and more empathetic.

Shared healing rituals further this sense of communal support, offering structured activities that help individuals process their grief while reinforcing community bonds. Group walks in honor of lost pets can be powerful, for example. These walks, perhaps through a local nature reserve or a well-loved park, allow participants to physically move through their grief together, surrounded by nature's calming influence. Similarly, organizing candlelight vigils where people can come together at dusk, light a candle, and share a moment of silence or a few words about their pet creates a shared sacred space of remembrance and reflection. These rituals provide not just solace but also a palpable sense of community support, which can be crucial for those who might otherwise feel isolated in their grief. The act of walking together or sharing the light of candles becomes a symbolic journey through grief, shared with others who understand the depth of the loss.

The rise of digital platforms has significantly transformed how communities can come together in mourning. Online tributes and social media play an increasingly vital role in creating virtual spaces where people from all over the world can share their grief and support one another. Dedicated online memorials on social media platforms, virtual candlelight vigils, or even live-streamed memorial services allow those who cannot be physically present to participate in the grieving process. These digital spaces offer unique advantages, such as the ability to connect with others regardless of geographical boundaries, and the opportunity for ongoing support. Posting a photo tribute of a beloved pet or sharing a particularly cherished memory can elicit supportive responses from a global community, providing comfort and solidarity. Moreover, these platforms often host specialized groups focused on pet loss, where resources, personal stories, and words of encouragement are shared daily, helping individuals feel less alone in their sorrow.

Building or finding a supportive community is essential to your recovery after pet loss. It's about recognizing that while the pain of loss is personal, the experience of grief can be mitigated by the support of others. Start by reaching out to local veterinarians, pet shops, or animal shelters to inquire about existing support groups or community events focused on pet loss. If none exist, consider taking the initiative to start one. Community centers often offer space for such gatherings, and creating flyers or social media posts can help spread the word. Be clear about the group's purpose to share memories, support each other, and perhaps engage in community projects like creating a memorial garden or organizing annual remembrance events. Such efforts not only aid in personal healing but also contribute to building a compassionate, understanding community that recognizes the significance of pet loss and offers a network of support for those grieving. Through these shared experiences and mutual understanding, the healing process becomes a collective endeavor, woven through the fabric of the community, strengthening and enriching it with empathy and shared human connection.

Pets Grieving Pets: Recognizing and Supporting Their Process

When a beloved pet passes away, the void they leave is felt not only by the human members of the family but often by their animal companions as well. Recognizing and supporting the grief experienced by surviving pets is a crucial aspect of managing the overall healing environment of your household. Pets, much like humans, can show signs of grief that may affect their behavior and overall well-being. Changes in behavior such as decreased interest in play, withdrawal from interaction, or altered eating and sleeping patterns can all be indicators that a pet is struggling with the loss of their companion. These signs can vary widely among animals, just as they do in people, depending on their unique personalities and the bond they shared with their departed friend. It's important for you, as a pet owner, to stay attuned to these changes and understand that they reflect a natural response to loss.

Supporting grieving pets involves several compassionate strategies that can help them adjust to the loss while maintaining their health and happiness. Maintaining routines is pivotal; consistent feeding times, walks, and bedtime can help provide a sense of structure and security for your pet during a confusing time. This regularity tells them that despite the changes, their daily life will still hold some familiarity. Additionally, offering extra attention and affection can help reassure them of your love and presence. Simple gestures like longer cuddling sessions, gentle grooming, or just sitting quietly together can significantly comfort a grieving pet. It's also beneficial to introduce new activities that can help distract them from their grief and stimulate their mind and body. This could be new toys, puzzle feeders that challenge them, or adventures to new parks for fresh sights and smells. These activities not only help to engage their senses but also foster opportunities for bonding between you and your pet, strengthening your connection during this shared period of adjustment.

The decision to introduce a new pet into the home after such a loss is a significant one and should be approached with careful consideration of the well-being of all animals involved. Timing is crucial; introducing a new pet too soon may confuse or stress your surviving pet, complicating their grieving process. It is generally wise to allow some time for your pet's behavior to return to normal levels and for your family to adjust to the new dynamics before bringing in another pet. When you feel the time might be right, consider your surviving pet's temperament and past reactions to new animals. Some pets might be more receptive to companions of different species or younger animals, while others might prefer a companion similar in age and energy level. When introducing a new pet, do so gradually and in controlled environments to ensure both animals can adjust comfortably to each other without overwhelming stress.

Involving surviving pets in memorializing activities can also be a soothing process for both you and your pet. This might include allowing them to be present during memorial services at home or visiting spots that were significant to your deceased pet. Some pet owners find it comforting to allow their pets to sniff an urn or other memorials, providing a sense of closure and understanding that their friend is gone and remembered with love. Sharing this space of grief and remembrance with your pet reinforces their importance in your life and acknowledges their role in the family, helping to strengthen the bond and support system within your home during this time of mutual adjustment.

Recognizing and supporting the grief of your surviving pets not only aids in their healing but also deepens your relationship with them, highlighting the profound interconnection between all members of a family, human and animal alike. By staying attentive and responsive to their needs, providing comfort, and gradually introducing new ways for them to find joy and companionship, you foster an environment where healing and love can continue to flourish.

Creating a Supportive Environment for Grieving Pet Owners

In the aftermath of a pet's passing, crafting a supportive environment can profoundly influence the grieving process, not just for you but for everyone around who feels the loss. Open communication is the cornerstone of such an environment. It's about creating a space where feelings and memories can be freely expressed without the fear of judgment. This openness allows individuals to share their grief, find common ground in their experiences, and support each other in ways that are genuinely empathetic and helpful. To foster this kind of communication, it's beneficial to set an example by sharing your own feelings and memories about the pet. This can encourage others to open up and can lead to a deeper, shared understanding of the loss, making the grieving process a collective, inclusive experience.

Educating those around you about the depth of grief associated with pet loss is also crucial. Many people may not realize how profound the loss of a pet can be, and they might inadvertently make comments or decisions that can seem dismissive. Taking the time to explain the bond you shared with your pet and the impact of their loss can help others understand your grief and offer more sensitive, appropriate support. This education isn't just about correcting misunderstandings but about fostering a deeper empathy that can strengthen relationships and build a more compassionate community. You might consider sharing articles, books, or other resources that articulate the complexities of pet loss grief, or even inviting them to attend a pet loss support group meeting with you, providing a firsthand look at how deeply others are affected too.

Experiencing grief in the workplace presents its own set of challenges and considerations. The professional environment often emphasizes productivity and efficiency, which can make expressing grief seem inappropriate or unprofessional. However, communicating your needs to your employer and coworkers can help in managing these challenges. Consider requesting a meeting with your HR department to discuss potential adjustments, such as flexible hours or the option to work from home temporarily. Being open about your loss can also inform your coworkers about your current state, allowing them to offer support or at least understand a change in your demeanor or performance.

It's helpful to articulate specific ways in which they can support you, whether it's needing a bit more patience on certain days or assistance with managing workload. This kind of communication helps prevent misunderstandings and builds a supportive work environment where you can grieve without the added stress of workplace conflicts or pressures. The importance of both seeking and offering support in times of grief cannot be overstated. On one hand, actively seeking support can provide you with the resources and comfort you need to navigate through your grief. This could involve reaching out to friends, family, or professionals who can offer empathy and guidance. On the other hand, offering support to others who are grieving can also be therapeutic. It can provide a sense of purpose and connection, reinforcing your own coping strategies and helping you to process your grief through the act of helping others.

Creating a reciprocal network of care enriches the supportive environment, making it a dynamic space of mutual understanding and aid. This network doesn't just help with coping with the loss of a pet; it strengthens community bonds and fosters a culture of empathy and support that can extend beyond the immediate grief.

Creating a supportive environment for grieving pet owners involves open communication, education, thoughtful workplace strategies, and a strong network of mutual support. These elements combine to form a compassionate backdrop against which the loss can be experienced and processed, not in isolation, but within a community that understands and shares the burden of grief. As this chapter integrates into the broader narrative of pet loss, it highlights the importance of collective support in healing and the significant role each person can play in creating a space where grief is respected and shared.

In wrapping up this chapter, we've explored various ways to support not just ourselves but also those around us in times of grief. From fostering open communication to educating others, proactively managing workplace dynamics to building supportive networks, these strategies are crucial in cultivating an environment where grief can be expressed and managed healthily. As we transition to the next chapter, we'll delve into the personal and collective journeys of healing, continuing to build on the foundation of support and understanding laid out here.

A Call For Help:

"One of the most important things you can do on this earth is to let people know they are not alone." - Shannon L. Alder

Pets provide us with so many wonderful things. Comfort, support, companionship, and unconditional love; the only expectation from our pets is that they be fed, sheltered, and loved. Your journey of healing has begun.

Now I ask you: What do we do about the family, man, woman, boy or girl who is still struggling with the loss of a beloved pet and companion? What if I told you that you can help them take their first steps toward the journey you've already embarked upon?

Our intent with "Comfort After Pet Loss Guide: Effectively Cope with Grief, Move Past Denial, Initiate Emotional Healing, Memorialize Your Beloved Pet and Get the Support You Need is simple: Help other pet owners get past the sorrow, grief, and pain suffered after the loss of dearly beloved pet and friend.

The next step is yours. We humbly request that you share what you've learned from reading this book thus far. Your voice can and will help others find peace and solace?

We implore you to take a few moments to write a review for this book. Share what you've learned and do your part to help others find their way forward after losing their pets.

Just a few sentences can make the difference between pain and comfort. Your review could be something like....

....a heartfelt guide to healing after pet loss

....a must read for pet owners

....a compassionate companion

....a beacon of hope during a challenging time

Ready to make a difference? Just scan the QR code below:

Chapter 6: Memorializing Your Pet

The loss of a pet carves a deep, tender space in our lives, a space once filled with the pitter-patter of paws and the soft, comforting presence of a creature who asked for nothing but love in return for their unconditional loyalty. As we navigate through the echoes of their absence, creating a memorial service stands as a poignant testament to the irreplaceable role they played in our lives. This chapter is dedicated to guiding you through the heartfelt process of planning a memorial service and ceremony that not only honors your pet's memory but also offers a space for collective mourning and healing.

Crafting a Personalized Memorial Service

Planning Details

When envisioning a memorial service that truly reflects the spirit of your cherished companion, every detail counts. It begins with choosing a location that resonates with personal significance, such as a favorite park where you walked your dog every morning, or your own backyard where your cat loved to lounge in the afternoon sun. The familiarity of the setting can evoke a sense of closeness and continuity, making the service feel more intimate and heartfelt. Selecting elements that mirror your pet's life enriches the ceremony, transforming it into a vibrant celebration of their unique traits and the joy they brought into your life. Consider incorporating their favorite blanket or toy, or perhaps setting up a display of photographs capturing key moments from their life. Each element should speak to the essence of your pet, weaving a narrative of their life that guests can connect with and remember.

Involving Loved Ones

The power of a communal grieving process cannot be understated. Inviting friends, family, and even surviving pets to partake in the memorial service can significantly enrich the experience. Each individual's presence adds a layer of love and shared memory that is both comforting and healing. Encourage attendees to share their own stories or anecdotes about your pet, perhaps through spoken words, written notes, or small symbolic gestures. These shared memories can paint a multifaceted picture of your pet's life, celebrated through the voices of those who knew them in different capacities. This collective remembrance not only helps in shouldering the weight of grief but also highlights the widespread impact your pet had on multiple lives, reaffirming their significance and cherished presence.

Memorial Service Activities

The activities during the service can vary widely, depending on what feels most appropriate for honoring your pet's memory. You might include a moment of silence, giving everyone a chance to reflect on their memories and the loss they feel. Alternatively, reading poems or passages that resonate with your feelings, or playing music that was significant to you and your pet, can evoke shared emotions and memories. These acts of collective expression not only help in personal healing but also create a shared space of emotional resonance that can be profoundly comforting to all present.

Creating a Memory Capsule

Introducing the idea of a memory capsule can provide a tangible way for attendees to contribute to the memorial. This capsule could be a beautiful box or container where guests can drop written notes, photos, or small mementos related to your pet. The act of placing these items into the capsule is symbolic, a way for each person to offer a part of their memory and relationship with your pet. Once sealed, the capsule can be kept in a special place in your home, buried under a newly planted tree in your garden, or another significant spot. Opening this capsule years later can serve as a beautiful reminder of your pet's life and the collective memories shared by friends and family, offering a lasting tribute that continues to honor your pet's legacy over time.

In crafting a personalized memorial service, you create not just a farewell to a beloved friend but a celebration of their life and the joy they shared with everyone around them. It's a process that, while steeped in sorrow, also brings about a sense of closure and communal healing, allowing you and others to remember and honor your pet in a deeply personal and meaningful way.

Keepsakes and Memorabilia: Tangible Memories

Creating keepsakes and memorabilia allows you to hold onto the physical essence of your pet, transforming everyday elements of their life into lasting symbols of love and remembrance. Selecting keepsakes often begins with considering what best captures the essence of your pet. Perhaps it's a paw print cast in clay, preserving the little details of their unique print, or a lock of fur, softly holding the color and texture that you loved to stroke. Personalized jewelry can also offer a discreet yet constant connection to your pet, such as a necklace incorporating their ashes or a bracelet engraved with their name. When choosing these keepsakes, think about what would feel most comforting to have close by, something that when seen or touched brings back warm, loving memories. It's these small, physical artifacts that can often bring the greatest comfort on days when your pet's absence feels particularly profound.

Displaying memorabilia in your home serves not only as a personal reminder of your pet but also as a way to keep their memory alive in your daily environment. Creating a dedicated space in your home for these items can serve as a sanctuary of sorts, a physical place where memories and presence feel concentrated. Consider setting up a small shelf or a corner of a room with your pet's photographs, their favorite toys, and other memorabilia. Arrange these items in a way that feels visually pleasing and emotionally comforting. Some people choose to create a more formal display, such as a shadow box or a glass cabinet, where items are preserved and arranged with care. This not only keeps the memories organized but also turns the display into a piece of art, a focal point in a room that invites reminiscence and reflection.

Sharing these memories and keepsakes with others who knew and loved your pet can be a deeply bonding experience. It allows those who shared in your pet's life to remember and celebrate that life together. You might choose to share stories about each keepsake, perhaps during gatherings or special occasions, explaining the significance behind each item. For instance, sharing the story of a holiday collar that your pet wore every Christmas can evoke shared laughter and fond memories. This act of sharing not only keeps the spirit of your pet alive but also strengthens the connections between those who share in the grief and celebration of your pet's life.

Legacy projects offer a creative and enduring way to compile these memories and highlight your pet's impact on your life. Creating a photo book or a memorial video are popular ways to capture and chronologically arrange the moments you shared with your pet. These projects can be deeply therapeutic to create, as they allow you to immerse yourself in the happy memories and the significant role your pet played in your life. Photo books can range from simple printed albums to elaborately designed pieces, complete with captions and quotes that reflect your feelings or share stories about the photos. Videos can include clips of your pet in their happiest moments, accompanied by music that either soothes or uplifts. The process of creating these legacy projects not only provides a therapeutic outlet for grief but also results in a beautiful homage to your pet, a keepsake that can be revisited and shared for years to come, ensuring that the love and joy they brought into your life are never forgotten.

Planting a Memorial Garden: Growth from Loss

Creating a memorial garden for your beloved pet offers a nurturing way to channel your grief into something beautiful that grows and flourishes over time, much like the love you shared with your pet. The process of choosing the right location for this garden involves careful consideration of several factors to ensure that the space is not only a tribute but also a personal sanctuary where you can reflect and find peace. Start by considering the visibility of the garden. You might prefer a quiet, secluded corner of your yard where you can feel close to your pet in privacy. Alternatively, choosing a more central area can make the garden a part of your daily life, a constant reminder of your pet's presence in your life. Accessibility is also crucial, especially if you plan to spend significant time in the garden. Ensure it is easily reachable, perhaps with a path that is gentle enough to walk on even in moments of deep contemplation or on days when the grief feels heavier.

Selecting plants for the garden can be a deeply personal choice, each plant holding significance that echoes the memory of your pet. You might choose plants that bloom around the time of year your pet was born or passed away, offering a natural marker of those significant dates. Consider also plants that attract wildlife, perhaps attracting the butterflies or birds your pet might have loved watching. The inclusion of such plants turns your garden into a lively, vibrant space, filled with life and a reminder of the cycles of the natural world, which can be comforting. For pets who had favorite smells or loved to nibble on certain herbs, including these can make the space feel more connected to their preferences, personalizing it further.

Incorporating physical memorials into your garden can enhance its significance, turning it into a landscape of memory. Engraved stones with your pet's name or a meaningful quote can be placed along the path or among the flowers, serving as reminders of the lessons and love your pet brought into your life. Sculptures or artworks that reflect your pet's personality or species can also add a unique touch, personalizing the space even more. Consider, for instance, a small statue of a cat lounging in the sun, or a custom wind chime that sings with the breeze, evoking the presence of your pet in a form that engages the senses. These elements invite not just reflection, but interaction, making the garden a dynamic tribute that engages the heart and soul.

The garden should ultimately serve as a healing space, a place where the beauty of the natural world soothes the pain of loss and fosters peace. Over time, tending to the garden can become a meditative practice, each act of care a way to nurture the memories of your pet. As plants grow, bloom, and change with the seasons, they mirror the process of grieving and healing, reminding you that with time, beauty can emerge from sorrow. This space becomes a testament to the cycle of life, growth, and renewal, offering a comforting reminder that love, like the garden, requires patience, care, and time to flourish. Here, in the quiet rustle of leaves and the serene patterns of growth and rest, you can find a living connection to your pet, a space where memories are tended and cherished in the ongoing dance of life and loss.

Digital Remembrance: Online Memorials and Tributes

In an age where digital connections often mirror our physical ones, the internet offers unique and heartfelt ways to remember pets who have passed away. Creating online memorials provides a space where memories can live on and be accessed from anywhere, at any time, allowing friends and family, no matter their location, to partake in the grieving and memorializing process. Various platforms and websites specialize in creating these digital memorials, ranging from dedicated pet memorial sites to more generalized platforms that allow for personal tributes. On these sites, you can create a beautiful, customized profile for your pet that includes photos, videos, and stories of your cherished moments together. You can also encourage others to contribute their memories and messages of love, creating a rich tapestry of shared experiences that celebrate your pet's life. This collective sharing can be incredibly comforting, knowing that your pet's impact on the world is recognized and cherished by others.

Social media platforms also play a significant role in how we share and commemorate the lives of our pets. These networks can serve as powerful tools for expressing grief and celebrating life. Sharing photos and stories of your pet can elicit support and understanding from your social media community, many of whom may have shared in your pet's life through the years. However, conquering social media during a time of grief requires a sense of balance and respect for your feelings and for those who might be engaging with your posts. It's helpful to share memories that invite interaction, such as prompting others to share their own stories of pets they have loved and lost, or asking for advice on coping with grief. These interactions can foster a sense of community and collective healing, making the vast digital space feel a bit warmer and more personal.

Virtual memorial services have emerged as a profound way to bridge physical distances, allowing friends and family from across the globe to come together and honor the memory of a pet. These services can be live-streamed through platforms that support video sharing and may include many of the traditional elements of a physical memorial service, such as eulogies, shared stories, and moments of silence. Participants can also contribute digitally, perhaps through a shared online photo album or a collaborative video montage that celebrates the pet's life. This format not only democratizes the grieving process, allowing anyone, anywhere, to participate, but also adapts to the modern need for flexibility and accessibility in how we commemorate our loved ones.

Engaging continually with online memorials can keep the memory of your pet alive and vibrant. Regular updates, such as posting on significant dates like the anniversary of your pet's adoption or passing, can help maintain a connection to the pet and provide ongoing comfort to you and others who shared in your pet's life. These posts can serve as reminders of your pet's lasting impact and the unconditional love they offered, ensuring that their memory continues to bring smiles and solace as time passes. This ongoing engagement not only keeps your pet's memory fresh but also reaffirms the lasting significance of the bond you shared, underscoring that while they may be gone, they are never forgotten.

Writing Your Pet's Story: A Legacy of Love

The act of writing your pet's story is much more than a mere recounting of events; it is a therapeutic endeavor that immortalizes the quirks, personality, and the precious moments you shared. This narrative, woven from your memories and emotions, not only serves as a personal keepsake but also as a bridge to connect with others who understand the depth of your attachment and loss. Writing about your pet allows you to capture the essence of their being. The tilt of their head, their playful antics, or the comfort found in their quiet companionship. As you begin to lay down words, you might find that what starts as a recounting of facts transforms into an emotional journey that celebrates their life and helps you navigate your grief.

Guidance on Writing

Embarking on writing your pet's story can seem daunting at first. You might wonder where to begin or how to structure such a narrative. Start with the simple memories, perhaps the day you brought your pet home, the special trips you took together, or the everyday moments that might seem mundane but are imbued with significant emotional weight. You can write in a free-form style, letting the memories flow as they come, or you might find it helpful to organize your thoughts chronologically or around specific themes or lessons your pet taught you. To ease into the process, consider using prompts such as, "My favorite memory of you is...", "I learned from you...", or "I miss when we used to...". These prompts can help you delve into the narrative, making the task less overwhelming and more guided. Whether you choose to write in a journal, compose blog posts, or draft a more structured story, each word you write strengthens the legacy of your pet, keeping their memory vibrant and alive.

Sharing the Story

Once your narrative takes shape, sharing your pet's story can be a powerful way to connect with others and honor your pet's memory. Family readings can be intimate gatherings where you read parts of your story, inviting others to remember and celebrate your pet's life together. These readings can open up conversations about grief, healing, and the joy that your pet brought into your lives, helping to process the loss collectively. If you're comfortable with a wider audience, consider publishing your story online or in print. Blog posts can reach fellow pet lovers across the globe, offering comfort and connection to those experiencing similar losses. For a more lasting tribute, compiling your writings into a book provides a tangible legacy that can be passed down to future generations, a testament to the love and lessons your pet left behind. Sharing your story not only keeps your pet's memory alive but also supports others in their grief, spreading understanding and compassion.

Story as a Legacy

Your pet's story is a mosaic of every joyous moment and every challenge overcome together, each piece a testament to the love shared. This narrative becomes a legacy, not just of the life lived but of the impact left on those who loved them. Writing this story is a way to ensure that your pet's personality, love, and lessons do not fade into the background of past memories but continue to influence and inspire. As you share these stories, you offer new insights into the depth of the bond between humans and pets, educating others and perhaps even encouraging them to open their homes and hearts to other animals in need of love. Moreover, your story stands as a beacon for others working through their paths of grief, showing them that while the pain of loss is profound, the beauty of the bond shared is everlasting, capable of reaching beyond the confines of life itself.

By crafting and sharing your pet's story, you create a lasting tribute that transcends the physical presence of your pet, transforming their memory into a source of eternal love and guidance. As these narratives unfold and connect us, they weave a collective tapestry of understanding, compassion, and shared history that enriches our lives and honors the pets who have left indelible marks on our hearts.

Annual Remembrance Rituals: Keeping Their Memory Alive

The passage of time following the loss of a beloved pet brings with it a mixture of sorrow and nostalgia, yet it also offers opportunities for honoring their memory in meaningful ways. Establishing annual rituals or traditions can transform the pain of absence into a celebration of the life shared, allowing you and others who knew your pet to remember them with love and gratitude each year. These rituals not only serve as heartfelt tributes to your pet but also as milestones in your own journey of healing and remembrance.

Creating these annual rituals might involve returning to activities or places that your pet enjoyed, imbuing these experiences with new significance. For example, if your pet loved nature, planting flowers each year on their birthday or the anniversary of their passing can become a nurturing act that symbolizes renewal and growth. Each bloom serves as a vibrant reminder of the joy your pet brought into your life. Alternatively, lighting candles can be a simple yet profound ritual, with each flame representing your ongoing love and the light your pet brought into your world. If there was a particular place where you and your pet spent happy times together, visiting this spot annually can evoke cherished memories and provide a sense of closeness. These rituals, by their very nature, offer comfort and continuity, helping to bridge the past with the present and future.

Involving friends, family, and even new pets in these annual remembrances can enhance the sense of community and shared memory.

Inviting those who knew and loved your pet to participate in these rituals can turn private remembrance into a communal celebration of your pet's life. Whether it's gathering together to plant flowers, share stories, or take a reflective walk in your pet's favorite park, these group activities can strengthen bonds between all who join in remembering. The collective presence of loved ones not only amplifies the emotional resonance of the rituals but also reinforces the communal support system, reminding everyone involved that they are not alone in their memories or their grief.

Personal reflection during these rituals provides a sacred space to navigate the complex emotions that anniversaries can evoke. Allowing yourself time to reflect on how your feelings have evolved can be enlightening, offering insights into your personal growth and healing process. It's also a time to acknowledge and embrace the range of emotions that might surface such as sadness for the loss, gratitude for the time shared, and peace with the passing of time. These moments of reflection can deepen your understanding of the ways your pet has shaped your life and how their memory continues to influence you. They serve as poignant reminders of the love you shared and the impact they had on your life, echoing through time.

Rituals serve as emotional anchors throughout our lives, providing stability and continuity in a world that is constantly changing. For those who have experienced the loss of a pet, these rituals become a vital connection to the past, a bridge to the memories shared with a beloved companion. They allow us to celebrate those memories, to mourn the loss, and to move forward with the reassurance that our pets are not forgotten. Through these annual rituals, we not only keep the memory of our pets alive but also integrate their legacy into our ongoing lives, ensuring that the love we shared continues to enrich and inspire us.

As we close this chapter on memorializing pets, we reflect on the various ways we can honor their memory. From creating tangible memorials and keepsakes to establishing meaningful rituals and sharing their stories. Each act of remembrance reinforces the bond we shared with our pets, keeping their spirit alive in our hearts and in the world around us. As we turn to the next chapter, we will explore how to embrace life after loss, finding ways to heal and to continue celebrating the joy and love our pets brought into our lives.

Chapter 7: Embracing Life After Loss

As the sun rises anew each day, so must we find ways to continue living fully, even in the wake of profound loss. Losing a cherished pet alters the very fabric of your daily life, leaving spaces that once brimmed with the joy and companionship of your beloved friend. As you face these quiet moments, the challenge becomes not only to find peace with the absence but to weave new patterns that honor your pet's memory while fostering personal growth and healing. This chapter seeks to guide you gently through redefining your everyday life, helping you fill the void left behind with activities and rituals that affirm the love you shared and encourage you to look forward with hope.

Redefining Your Daily Routine Without Your Pet

Adjusting Daily Routines

The routine you shared with your pet likely structured your day. Morning walks, feeding times, and playful evenings shaped your schedule and brought rhythm to your life. With your pet's passing, the structure may crumble, leaving a sense of disarray. To regain balance, consider gently reshaping these routines. If mornings feel particularly empty without your pet, you might start your day with a new ritual, like a quiet coffee on the porch, allowing yourself space to reflect and appreciate the new day. Alternatively, replacing the usual walk time with a jog or a bike ride can maintain the routine while introducing a new activity that benefits your well-being. It's important to integrate activities that not only fill the time but also provide emotional or physical benefits, helping to mend the gap left in your daily life.

Filling the Void

The void your pet leaves is not merely physical but deeply emotional. Engaging in hobbies or activities can play a crucial role in managing the weight of this emptiness. Creative pursuits like painting or writing can be particularly therapeutic, providing an outlet for your emotions and a way to express the love and nostalgia you feel. Physical activities such as yoga or gardening can also help by improving your mental health and keeping you connected to the living world. Consider dedicating a part of your garden to your pet, planting flowers or a tree in their memory, which can offer a living tribute that grows and flourishes, much like the memories you hold dear.

Creating New Traditions

New traditions can serve as bridges between the past and the present, honoring your pet's memory while allowing you to move forward. These might include annual events such as a remembrance day on your pet's adoption anniversary or birthday, where you might light a candle, share stories, or look through photos. These traditions can be as public or private as you feel comfortable with, perhaps involving family and friends who knew your pet or simply a personal moment of reflection. The key is to create rituals that feel meaningful and provide comfort, reinforcing the continuing impact your pet has on your life.

Balancing Remembrance and Moving Forward

The delicate balance between honoring the memory of your pet and embracing the future can be challenging. It is healthy to remember and celebrate your pet's life, but it is equally important to allow yourself to experience joy and new experiences without guilt. Integrating remembrance into your life in a way that feels natural and positive is crucial. For instance, you might keep a framed photo of your pet in a lively part of your house, symbolizing their continued presence in your life. Simultaneously, open your home and heart to new experiences and relationships and remember these are not replacements but expansions of your capacity to love and cherish. Remember, moving forward does not mean leaving behind; it means letting the love and lessons learned from your pet guide you into new chapters of your life, enriched by their memory.

In redefining your daily routine without your pet, the journey is about finding the proper balance. One that honors the past while embracing the present and future. It involves adjusting your daily activities, filling the emotional void left behind, introducing meaningful new traditions, and finding a harmonious balance between remembrance and forward movement. Each step, each new routine, and each tradition is a step towards healing, a testament to the resilience of the human spirit and the enduring impact of the love we share with our pets. As you integrate these changes into your life, may you find peace and a renewed sense of joy, carrying the legacy of your beloved pet forward with every step.

The Role of Legacy in Healing

Legacy, in the context of a beloved pet who has passed, transcends mere memory. It embodies the enduring impact your pet had on your life and the lives of those around you. This legacy can manifest in myriad forms, ranging from the continuation of shared rituals to the establishment of projects that channel your grief into positive actions. For many pet owners, understanding that their love and care can extend beyond the physical presence of their pet offers a profound source of comfort and purpose. It's about creating something lasting, something that not only commemorates the life of your pet but also perpetuates the love and care they inspired.

Projects that build on the legacy of your pet can provide a tangible means of channeling your grief and transforming it into actions that reflect the joy and love your pet brought into your life. For instance, starting a charity or setting up a fund in your pet's name to support animal welfare can be an impactful way to extend the compassion you showed to your pet to others in need. Such initiatives not only honor your pet's memory but also create a ripple effect of kindness and care, touching the lives of many other animals and people. Alternatively, creating a piece of art, whether it's a sculpture in your garden or a painted portrait that hangs in your living room, can serve as a daily reminder of your pet's spirit and personality. These creative expressions not only help in processing grief but also celebrate the unique aspects of your pet's life that brought you joy.

Focusing on these legacy projects can significantly aid in the healing process by providing you with a sense of purpose and continuity. Engaging in activities that reflect the love you felt for your pet helps bridge the gap between the past and the present, allowing you to carry forward their legacy in meaningful ways. It transforms the relationship from one of presence to one of enduring impact, where the love and lessons your pet imparted continue to influence and inspire. This shift in focus from loss to legacy can be incredibly empowering, turning the act of remembrance into a dynamic engagement with life and the community around you.

The importance of sharing your pet's legacy cannot be overstated. By involving friends, family, and even the wider community in legacy projects or remembrances, you create a communal space for healing and memory that enriches everyone's understanding of loss and recovery. Hosting an annual event to raise funds for the charity established in your pet's name, for instance, not only keeps their memory alive but also strengthens community ties through shared goals and collaborative efforts. These shared activities encourage conversations about grief and healing, allowing others to express their feelings and share in the communal process of remembering and celebrating your pet's life. This collective participation in legacy projects reinforces the communal fabric, offering multiple perspectives on loss while highlighting the universal experiences of love, grief, and remembrance.

In essence, the legacy of a beloved pet provides a narrative thread that weaves through your life and the lives of others, continuing to tell a story of love, care, and transformative impact. As you engage with these legacy projects, you honor the past while actively shaping a future enriched by the lessons and love your pet left behind. This ongoing engagement with legacy not only helps heal the heart but also ensures that the love shared with your pet continues to inspire and influence long after they have gone. As you move forward, let these acts of remembrance and creation guide you, offering not only solace but also a way to celebrate the indelible mark your pet has left on your life and the world.

Opening Your Heart: When to Consider Another Pet

When the echoes of paws on your floor have faded, and the heart begins to heal, you might find yourself contemplating the pitter-patter of new four-legged friends. Deciding when to welcome another pet into your home is a journey marked by reflection on readiness and respect for the past you cherished with your previous companion. Assessing emotional readiness is crucial; it's about ensuring your heart has enough room for new love without feeling overshadowed by grief. Signs that you might be ready include finding yourself reminiscing about the joy of pet companionship more than the pang of loss, or when you start seeing pet toys in the store and think about how much joy they would bring to a new furry friend, rather than just a reminder of what was lost.

However, readiness isn't just about overcoming sadness. It's about being able to look back at your time with your previous pet with fondness and peace, rather than overwhelming sorrow. If memories bring smiles more often than tears, it might be time to consider opening your home to another pet. It's also important to consider your lifestyle and whether you can commit the time, energy, and resources needed to care for another pet. This reflection ensures that any decision to adopt again is made in the best interest of both you and the potential new pet.

Honoring the memory of your lost pet while embracing the future with another involves complex emotions, often mingled with feelings of guilt or betrayal. It's vital to acknowledge these feelings and understand that loving another pet does not diminish the love you had for your previous one. Creating a space in your heart and home for a new pet can be seen as a tribute to the love you shared with your former companion, a testament to how they taught you the value and depth of pet companionship. Framing the arrival of a new pet as a continuation of your capacity to give and receive love can ease feelings of guilt and help you see this step as positive both for you and the memory of your pet.

Choosing a new pet involves thoughtful consideration of several factors to ensure a good match. Think about the temperament that would best fit your current lifestyle. For instance, a high-energy puppy might be perfect if you're active and have time for training, but an older, calmer dog might be better suited if you're looking for a low-maintenance companion. Consider also how a new pet would fit into the legacy of the pet who has passed. Perhaps adopting from the same shelter or rescue organization, or choosing a breed similar to your previous pet, can serve as a link between your past and future pet experiences. However, it's also okay to choose differently, as each pet has its own unique place in your life.

Integrating a new pet into your family, especially if you have other pets who are still grieving, requires careful planning and sensitivity. Start by introducing the new pet gradually, allowing your existing pets to adjust to their presence in a controlled, calm environment. Use neutral spaces for initial meetings to avoid territorial responses. Scent swapping, such as using blankets or toys, before face-to-face meetings can help familiarize your pets with each other indirectly. Monitoring interactions and adjusting the pace of integration based on the comfort levels of all animals involved ensures a smoother transition. This thoughtful approach not only respects the grieving process of your existing pets but also sets a foundation for positive future relationships within your pet family.

Welcoming a new pet is not about replacing the one you lost but about expanding the circle of love in your life. It's a step forward that honors the past while embracing the future, filled with new joys and the continued comfort of companionship. As you consider this step, let your memories and the lessons learned from your lost pet guide you, ensuring that the love you continue to offer is a reflection of the love you've known.

Fostering or Volunteering: Giving Back in Your Pet's Honor

When the silence of a home once filled with the bustling energy of a beloved pet becomes overwhelming, engaging in activities like fostering or volunteering can introduce a new kind of fulfillment into your life. Fostering animals provides a temporary home to pets in need, offering them the love and stability they require until they can find permanent homes. This act of caregiving can significantly aid your healing process, as it allows you to pour the love still residing in your heart into the care of other animals. The benefits of fostering extend beyond providing essential care to animals; it helps mend the broken pieces of your heart. Each animal you help can bring a renewed sense of purpose and joy into your life, reminding you of the happiness that caring for a pet can bring. It's a poignant way to honor the memory of your pet, continuing the legacy of love and care that they inspired in you.

Moreover, fostering can also help mitigate the loneliness that often accompanies the loss of a pet. The presence of a foster pet in your home can bring a comforting sense of companionship, filling your days with purpose and activity. The routines of feeding, playing, and caring for them can restore a sense of normalcy and structure to your daily life, helping you adjust to life without your pet while still being surrounded by the love of an animal. It's important, however, to be aware of your emotional state and readiness to foster. Ensure that you view fostering as a positive addition to your life, not as a replacement for your lost pet, and that you are emotionally stable enough to handle the responsibilities and eventual goodbye as they move on to permanent homes.

Volunteering at animal shelters or other pet welfare organizations is another enriching way to give back in honor of your pet. Many organizations rely heavily on volunteers for everything from administrative tasks to direct animal care, and offering your time can make a significant impact. This involvement not only helps the animals but also connects you with a community of like-minded individuals who share your passion for animal welfare. Engaging with others who recognize and appreciate the value of each animal's life can reinforce your own feelings of purpose and contribution, providing a supportive network that understands the profound bond between humans and animals. Volunteering allows you to be a part of something larger than yourself, a collective effort that makes a real difference in the lives of many animals, serving as a living tribute to the memory of your pet.

The emotional considerations involved in fostering or volunteering after experiencing pet loss are significant. It is essential to approach these activities with a clear understanding of your emotional boundaries and current state. If you find yourself overwhelmed by sadness, it might be helpful to start slowly, perhaps volunteering just a few hours a week or fostering only one pet at a time. It's also crucial to acknowledge and respect your feelings throughout the process. If at any point the experience stirs up emotions that are too difficult to handle, it may be necessary to step back and reassess your readiness to continue. Remember, it's perfectly okay to set limits and progress at your own pace; your well-being is just as important as the help you are providing to the animals.

Giving back through fostering or volunteering creates a positive impact not just in the lives of numerous animals, but also within your own life. By dedicating time and love to animals in need, you actively contribute to the wellbeing of the pet community, ensuring that your actions create ripples of kindness and care. This involvement is a powerful way to honor the memory of your pet, extending the love they gave you to others who need it just as much. As you give of yourself in these ways, you not only keep your pet's memory alive but also build upon the legacy of compassion and care that they inspired. Whether you choose to foster, volunteer, or engage in both, these acts of kindness forge a path of healing and purpose, allowing you to transform your grief into actions that celebrate life and offer new beginnings to those in need.

Keeping the Bond Alive: Honoring Your Pet in Everyday Life

As days turn to weeks and weeks to months, the presence of a beloved pet can still resonate deeply within the spaces they once filled. Keeping their memory vibrant and alive need not be confined to specific rituals or anniversaries; it can seamlessly integrate into the very fabric of your daily life. Simple yet profound, everyday reminders can serve as gentle nudges of the bond you shared, providing comfort and continuity. One such way is through personal adornments, such as wearing a piece of jewelry that holds symbolic significance, or a pendant containing their image or a bracelet engraved with their name. These items, carried close to your body, serve as constant, comforting reminders of their presence. Similarly, carrying a small token, such as a keychain made from their collar or a pocket-sized stone from your favorite walking path, can provide a tactile reminder of their enduring presence in your life.

Incorporating memories of your pet into your daily routines can transform mundane activities into moments of remembrance and honor. For instance, if morning walks were a cherished routine with your pet, continue these walks in their honor, perhaps taking routes that were especially enjoyed or meaningful. During these walks, allow yourself moments of reflection on the joyous times spent together, or simply speak to your pet in your heart, updating them on your life's happenings. This practice keeps their memory actively part of your everyday life and can bring a sense of peace and continuity. Similarly, if your evenings were once spent with your pet by your side, you might dedicate this time to relaxing near a special place you've created in their memory, such as a favorite chair with their picture placed beside it, or a small altar with items that were significant to them.

Engaging in continued conversations about your pet with friends and family can also play a crucial role in keeping their memory alive. Sharing stories of your pet not only keeps their spirit alive but also allows for communal healing and memory-sharing. These narratives can be joyous, reflective, or even humorous, as they celebrate the life and antics of your beloved companion. Encourage family members or friends to recount their favorite memories, or perhaps share how your pet impacted their lives. This shared storytelling not only honors your pet but also strengthens the bonds between those who knew and loved them, creating a collective memory that keeps their spirit vibrant within the community.

Finally, living in a way that honors the memory of your pet can have profound implications for your personal development and interactions with the world. Pets often teach us about unconditional love, patience, and the joy of simple pleasures. Embody these lessons in your daily interactions and choices. Practice kindness and patience, whether with yourself or others, reflecting the compassion your pet showed you. Engage in activities that bring joy and peace, whether it's spending time in nature, volunteering, or simply taking moments to be present and grateful. By living in a way that reflects the best qualities of your pet, you not only honor their memory but also spread the love and positivity they brought into your life to those around you.

Through these daily reminders, incorporated memories, shared stories, and life choices that reflect the lessons learned from your beloved pet, their memory continues to enrich your life. These practices ensure that the love you shared remains a vibrant and nurturing force, guiding you gently as you navigate the path ahead, imbued with their enduring spirit and love.

Growth and Transformation: Finding Meaning After Loss

The loss of a beloved pet undeniably marks an end, but within this ending, there are seeds of new beginnings that hold the potential for personal transformation and growth. As you navigate through the grief, you might discover an increased capacity for empathy, resilience, and a deeper understanding of life's fragile cycles. These qualities often emerge from the depths of sorrow, shaped by the love and loss experienced, offering you a new lens through which to view the world around you. For instance, the empathy developed through understanding your pet's needs can heighten your sensitivity to the emotions of others, enriching your relationships and interactions. This heightened empathy can lead you to engage more deeply with friends, family, or even strangers, fostering connections that are both richer and more rewarding.

Resilience, too, is often forged in the fires of loss. Each day that you find the strength to move forward, you build a reserve of inner toughness that can help you face future challenges with a steadier heart. This resilience is a testament to your capacity to endure heartache and emerge stronger, a direct reflection of the love and care you invested in your pet. Understanding the cycles of life, including loss, also instills a profound appreciation for the present moment and the impermanence of life's stages. This awareness can encourage you to live more fully, embracing each moment with the recognition that now is the time to love, act, and engage with the world around you.

Finding new meaning in life after the loss of a pet involves channeling your grief into pursuits or causes that ignite passion and purpose. Consider what your pet loved or what made them unique, and seek out activities that align with these passions. If your dog loved being outdoors, perhaps take up hiking or environmental conservation as a way to honor their memory. If your cat was rescued, getting involved in animal welfare or rescue organizations can be a fitting tribute. Engaging in these activities allows you to transform your sorrow into positive action, creating a legacy of care that continues the love you and your pet shared.

This transformation through grief is not just about personal change but about how these changes can impact the world around you. As you learn and grow from your experiences of love and loss, you carry forward a legacy of learning that can influence and inspire others. The lessons of patience, unconditional love, and joy that pets teach us can inform your actions and relationships, encouraging a more compassionate, thoughtful approach to life. Sharing these lessons with others, whether through storytelling, community involvement, or personal interactions, extends the impact of your pet's life beyond their physical presence, contributing to a broader narrative of healing and growth.

Embracing the growth and transformation that can come from the loss of a beloved pet will require you to step into a renewed version of yourself that will carry forward the best qualities of the bond you shared. This new chapter of your life, enriched by the lessons of love and loss, offers a path that is both healing and transformative, allowing you to contribute to the world in ways that honor the memory of your pet and the love you continue to hold for them. As this chapter closes, remember that the journey of grief and growth is not just about enduring loss but about embracing the opportunities for deep, meaningful engagement with life that this loss unveils.

Chapter 8: Building Resilience for the Future

I n the quiet aftermath of pet loss, where the echoes of a beloved companion's presence linger, lies an opportunity for profound personal growth and resilience. The journey through grief, while deeply personal and often fraught with challenges, also paves the way for a renewed understanding of the cyclical nature of life and relationships. As you emerge from the initial intensity of grief, you may find yourself reflecting on the lessons learned from your past experiences with pet loss, each one contributing to a stronger, more resilient future self. This chapter delves into how these past experiences prepare you for future relationships with pets, enhancing your capacity to love, understand, and eventually, let go with grace.

Reflecting on Past Losses

Every pet that graces our lives leaves an indelible mark on our hearts, and with each loss, a wealth of lessons is left behind. Reflecting on these lessons is more than an act of remembrance, it's a process that fosters emotional resilience, turning sorrow into wisdom. You might recall how the loss of a childhood pet taught you the reality of mortality, a tough but essential lesson that helped you appreciate the transient beauty of life. Or perhaps, the recent passing of a beloved cat or dog highlighted the importance of compassionate care and presence during their final days, teaching you about the power of empathy and the strength required to make difficult decisions with kindness and respect for life.

In this reflection, you're encouraged to explore not only the emotional impact of these losses but also the coping strategies that helped you navigate through the grief. Was it the support of friends and family, the solace found in memorializing your pet, or perhaps the therapeutic effect of writing about your feelings? Understanding what helped you in the past can fortify your emotional toolkit, preparing you for future losses and reinforcing your capacity to recover and find joy again.

Visual Element: Reflective Journaling Prompts

To aid in this reflective process, consider keeping a journal where you can explore your feelings and memories associated with each pet you have loved and lost. Here are some prompts to guide your writing:

- What is the most valuable lesson you learned from each pet you have lost?

- How did you cope with each loss at the time, and what coping mechanisms were most effective?

- How has each loss shaped your understanding of life, relationships, and grief?

Applying Lessons to Future Relationships

The insights gained from past pet relationships are invaluable when forging new bonds with future pets. Each relationship with a pet is a learning experience, teaching us more about the needs of different animals and refining our ability to care for them. For instance, understanding the subtle signs of distress or illness in one pet can make you more attuned to future pets' health and well-being, enabling you to act swiftly and confidently when needed.

Moreover, the emotional resilience developed through past losses enhances your capacity to fully engage with new pets, even in the knowledge of eventual loss. This resilience allows you to embrace the joy and companionship of new pets with an open heart, enriched by the understanding that while the pain of loss is inevitable, the love shared is worth the sorrow. By applying the lessons of empathy, patience, and unconditional love learned from past pets, you can deepen the bonds with new companions, creating relationships that are both fulfilling and healing.

Preparedness for Future Losses

Part of building resilience for the future involves preparing emotionally for the inevitable losses that come with loving pets. Accepting the natural cycle of life and death is crucial in this preparation. It involves acknowledging from the outset that the time with your pet is limited, which can profoundly change how you experience and value the relationship. This acceptance doesn't diminish the joy or love shared but rather enhances your appreciation for the present moments. It encourages a mindfulness that cherishes every day spent with your pet, knowing that these moments are both precious and fleeting.

Emotional preparation also includes understanding the stages of grief and recognizing the personal signs of your grieving process. Knowing how you are likely to react to loss, based on past experiences, can help you better manage your emotions and seek appropriate support when the time comes. It's about creating a mental and emotional framework that acknowledges grief as a natural, albeit painful, part of life, equipping you with the tools to navigate it with grace and self-compassion.

Gratitude for Shared Time

Finally, fostering a sense of gratitude for the time shared with your pets can profoundly affect your resilience. Each relationship with a pet offers unique joys, challenges, and unconditional love, enriching your life and teaching you about mutual care and respect. By focusing on gratitude for these gifts, rather than solely on the loss, you shift your perspective from what is gone to what was gained. This shift doesn't negate the pain of loss but embeds it within a larger context of love and enrichment, celebrating the life shared rather than mourning the loss alone.

Embracing gratitude helps to soften the sharp edges of grief, allowing you to move forward with a heart full of love and appreciation for the companionship you were privileged to enjoy. It turns memories into treasures, moments into lessons, and relationships into legacies, weaving them into the fabric of your life as sources of strength, joy, and inspiration. As you continue to navigate your path forward, let these reflections guide you, fortifying your resilience and enriching your relationships with every step you take into the future.

Building a Support System for Future Grief

Moving past grief necessitates a solid support system and a network of understanding hearts and hands that can hold you up when the emotional tides run high. Building this network is less about gathering numbers and more about cultivating depth and understanding in relationships, ensuring that when the time comes, you're surrounded by individuals who truly grasp the nuances of your sorrow. This involves identifying empathetic friends, family members, and professionals who have either walked similar paths themselves or possess a natural capacity for empathy and support.

Creating such a network means being intentional about whom you spend your time with and whom you confide in about your pet losses. Start by evaluating your current relationships. Consider who has been understanding about pet loss in the past or has shown a capacity for deep emotional support during other challenging times. These are the people likely to stand steadfast beside you in future grief. Moreover, it helps to extend this network to include professionals such as therapists or counselors who specialize in grief, particularly pet loss. Their expertise can not only provide emotional support but also equip you with strategies to manage grief more effectively.

Role of Community

Beyond your immediate circle, the broader community plays a crucial role in providing support and understanding. This can include online communities and local support groups specifically geared toward pet loss. Online platforms offer the advantage of accessing support at any time, which can be particularly helpful during moments of acute grief that can occur unpredictably. These platforms often provide a space to share stories, memories, and strategies for coping with loss, connecting you with others who can relate to your experience on a visceral level.

Local support groups, on the other hand, offer the irreplaceable benefit of face-to-face interaction. Being physically present with others who understand pet loss can foster a profound sense of community and shared healing. These groups often meet regularly and can provide a structured approach to dealing with grief, including sessions led by grief counselors, shared memorial activities, or group discussions that can help normalize your feelings and provide diverse perspectives on managing grief.

Proactive Communication

As important as it is to build a support network, equally crucial is your ability to communicate proactively with this network about your needs and preferences during times of grief. This proactive communication involves being open about what type of support you find most helpful, whether it's having someone to listen as you share memories of your pet, receiving practical help with daily tasks, or just having company. Letting your network know how they can best support you helps prevent feelings of isolation and ensures that the support provided is effective and meaningful.

It's also beneficial to communicate your preferred methods for checking in; some might prefer phone calls, while others might find texts or emails less intrusive. Clarifying these preferences can help your support network be more considerate and responsive in ways that truly help, ensuring that their intentions to support align effectively with your comfort and needs.

Support Resources

To enhance this network of support, it's beneficial to compile a list of resources that you can access during times of need. This list can include hotlines for immediate emotional support, counseling services that specialize in grief, and contact information for local pet loss support groups. Additionally, include resources that offer practical advice on dealing with the loss, such as websites or books that focus on pet bereavement. Keeping this list easily accessible ensures that you can quickly find support when you need it most.

By building a robust support system, you equip yourself with a safety net of empathetic and practical resources that can help ease the journey through grief. This network not only provides emotional solace but also strengthens your resilience, ensuring that you are supported and understood as you navigate the complexities of loss and healing. As you continue to foster these relationships and resources, remember that each connection, each conversation, and each shared moment of understanding adds a layer of strength to your foundation of resilience, preparing you to face future challenges with a community of support at your back.

Chapter 9: Emotional Preparedness

Understanding the Life Cycle of Pets

In Chapter 8 we discussed building resilience for the future, now we take hold of the present. Grasping the natural life cycle of our cherished companions, from playful puppies and kittens to their dignified golden years, is a cornerstone in nurturing a relationship founded on realistic expectations and deep understanding. When you bring a pet into your life, awareness of their potential lifespan and the health challenges they may face as they age is crucial. This knowledge not only prepares you for the practical aspects of pet care but also cushions the emotional impact as they grow older. For instance, knowing that certain breeds of dogs or cats are prone to specific health issues allows you to monitor these conditions proactively, seek timely veterinary care, and adjust their environment to better suit their changing needs. It also sets a realistic timeline for your shared life, enabling you to cherish every moment and make informed decisions when it comes to their health and quality of life.

Deeper than the practicality of understanding your pet's potential health trajectory, there's the emotional preparation that comes with this knowledge. Developing acceptance of the natural life cycle of your pets includes coming to terms with the inevitability of aging and death. While it's a topic many pet owners may shy away from, early acceptance can profoundly affect the quality of the relationship with your pet. It fosters a mindset that values quality over quantity, prompting you to make the most of the time you have together. This acceptance is not about resignation but about appreciation. It encourages you to live fully in the present with your pet, creating meaningful experiences that celebrate their life, rather than constantly fearing the future.

Building emotional resilience in the face of these realities is vital. It involves cultivating a mindset equipped to handle the ups and downs of pet ownership, from the joyous moments of youth to the more challenging times of health issues and aging. Mindfulness practices can play a significant role here. Engaging in daily mindfulness with your pet, perhaps during walks or quiet cuddling sessions, can enhance your awareness of the present moment, helping you appreciate the simple joys of their companionship. These practices also teach you to manage your emotions more effectively, providing a calm anchor in moments of stress or sadness related to your pet's health or behavior changes.

Pre-Loss Grief: Addressing Anticipatory Grief

Anticipatory grief is a profound, often overlooked aspect of pet ownership. It begins the moment you recognize that your pet's time with
you may be drawing to a close, whether due to aging or a terminal
illness. This type of grief can be confusing; it carries all the hallmarks
of traditional mourning, sadness, denial, and bargaining; but your pet
is still here. You might find yourself mourning their loss even while
they lie beside you. To successfully move forward requires sensitivity
and a proactive approach to maintaining both your mental health and
the quality of life for your pet.

One effective strategy to manage anticipatory grief is to focus on
creating a comfortable and loving environment for your aging or ill
pet. This could involve adjusting their diet, modifying your home to
accommodate their physical limitations, or increasing their comfort
with extra bedding or pain management under veterinary supervision.
Taking these practical steps can provide a sense of control and purpose, helping you focus on the present responsibilities rather than the
impending loss.

Moreover, it's essential to seek support during this challenging time.
Connecting with online forums, support groups, or friends who have
been through similar experiences can provide comfort and practical
advice. Sharing your feelings and fears about your pet's decline can
help alleviate the sense of isolation that often accompanies anticipatory grief. Additionally, professional help from a counselor who
specializes in pet loss can offer valuable guidance on how to cope with
these complex emotions.

As you face the reality of your pet's life cycle, from vibrant youth to dignified old age, embracing both the joys and the challenges can enhance your resilience and deepen the bond you share. By educating yourself on what to expect, accepting the natural progression of life, and engaging in practices that anchor you in the present, you prepare not only to handle the inevitable with grace but also to appreciate the profound journey of companionship your pet offers.

The Importance of Self-Compassion in Resilience

When the waves of grief wash over you after the loss of a beloved pet, the instinct might be to remain stoic, to suppress the pain or rush through the healing process. However, embracing self-compassion during these moments can be your greatest ally, transforming the way you navigate the emotional tumult. Self-compassion is the art of treating yourself with the same kindness and understanding that you would offer a good friend in distress. It acknowledges that suffering, failure, and imperfection are part of the shared human experience.

Practicing self-compassion begins with recognizing that it's okay not to be okay. It's about allowing yourself to feel whatever emotions are surfacing such as sadness, anger, and confusion without judgment. This might mean taking a day off when the grief feels overwhelming or indulging in a comfort activity that soothes your spirit. It's acknowledging that grief doesn't follow a neat, predictable path and that healing takes time. When you're kind to yourself, you're more likely to recover from setbacks and maintain emotional resilience. This resilience isn't about never falling, but about how gently you pick yourself up when you do.

Incorporating specific self-care strategies that foster self-compassion can make a significant difference in your healing journey. Setting boundaries is a critical aspect of this. It might involve choosing not to attend social events that feel too demanding in the wake of your loss or setting limits on how much grief-related conversation you can handle with others. Self-affirmations can also play a transformative role. Simple, positive statements that reinforce your worth and the normalcy of your grief can fortify your mental and emotional defenses. For example, reminding yourself, "It's okay to feel sad," or "I am doing the best I can," helps validate your feelings and encourages a compassionate internal dialogue.

Seeking joy might seem counterintuitive during grief, but it's a vital part of nurturing self-compassion. Joy acts as a counterbalance to the weight of sadness, providing moments of relief and perspective. This could be as simple as watching a favorite movie, spending time in nature, or enjoying a meal with loved ones. These activities don't negate your grief but offer a reminder that joy and sorrow can coexist, and embracing both can lead to a more balanced emotional state.

Overcoming Self-Judgment

One of the more insidious aspects of grief is the self-judgment that often accompanies it. You might chastise yourself for not "being stronger," or for not "moving on" quickly enough, as if there's a standard timeline for healing. This self-criticism only deepens the pain, creating a cycle of negative self-talk that can hinder your healing process. Overcoming this self-judgment is crucial for fostering resilience and embracing a healthier grieving process.

Start by recognizing that grief is a deeply personal experience and that everyone reacts differently. There's no "right" way to grieve, and there's no universal timeline for healing. When you catch yourself falling into self-criticism, pause and reflect on what you would say to a friend in a similar situation. You would likely offer words of comfort and support, not criticism. Try to extend the same compassion to yourself. This might involve actively challenging negative thoughts when they arise and replacing them with more compassionate perspectives. For instance, if you think, "I should be over this by now," remind yourself, "I'm healing at my own pace, and that's okay."

Documenting these thoughts and the responses you'd like to cultivate can also be helpful. Keeping a journal where you track instances of self-judgment and actively reframe them can not only provide insight into patterns of negative thinking but also allow you to see your progress towards more self-compassionate responses.

Compassion as a Strength

Redefining compassion as a strength rather than a weakness is pivotal in changing how you view and experience grief. Compassion, including self-compassion, is often seen as a soft or even a disadvantageous trait in a culture that prizes stoicism and quick recovery from setbacks. However, embracing compassion can significantly enhance your resilience, equipping you with the emotional flexibility to handle life's challenges more effectively.

Compassion allows you to hold space for your pain, understanding it as a part of life rather than something to be feared or avoided. This openness not only alleviates the suffering but also deepens your empathy for others experiencing similar losses. It fosters a sense of connectedness, reducing feelings of isolation and enhancing your support network. Moreover, by viewing compassion as a strength, you empower yourself to face future losses with a more grounded and balanced approach. You know that you can handle pain with grace and that kindness towards yourself and others is not a liability but a profound source of strength.

By cultivating self-compassion, challenging self-judgment, and re-defining compassion as a strength, you equip yourself with the tools not only to survive the grief of losing a pet but to thrive beyond it. These practices forge a path through the pain, transforming the journey of grief into an opportunity for growth and deep, meaningful resilience. As you continue to integrate these practices into your life, they become second nature, a default setting that colors your interactions with yourself and the world with a richer, more compassionate hue.

Creating a Legacy of Love: How to Continue Honoring Lost Pets

When we think about legacies, what often comes to mind are the tangible remnants left behind. But when it comes to the cherished pets we've lost, the legacy is less about physical artifacts and more about the profound ways they've shaped our lives and perspectives. This legacy is not static; it's a living, breathing continuation of the love you shared, manifested through your actions and choices. Embracing the concept of a living legacy means finding ways to express and embody the love, joy, and lessons your pet brought into your life, ensuring that their impact extends far beyond their physical presence.

One powerful way to honor your pet's memory is through undertaking legacy projects that create positive change in the world. These projects can be as diverse as the personalities of the pets we've loved. For instance, if your dog loved nothing more than a day at the park, initiating a community project to clean up and maintain local parks can be a fitting tribute. This not only improves your community but also creates a space that other pets and owners can enjoy, spreading the joy that your pet brought into your life. Alternatively, if your pet was a rescue animal, establishing a fund or volunteering for animal shelters can help other animals find the same happiness your pet found with you. These acts of service extend the love you experienced with your pet, making a tangible impact in the world in their name.

Passing on the love you received from your pet to others is another heartfelt way to keep their memory alive. This doesn't necessarily mean adopting more pets, though that might be part of it. Instead, consider embodying the unconditional love and patience your pet showed you. You might find opportunities to share this love in everyday interactions, volunteering, or supporting friends and family through their challenging times. Each act of kindness and understanding is a thread in the larger tapestry of your pet's legacy, woven through your life and the lives of those around you.

Documenting the legacy of your pet can also play a crucial role in preserving and sharing the love you shared. This could take the form of writing a book or blog posts that recount your journey together, the challenges you faced, and the joy you shared. These stories can serve as comfort to others finding their way through the pain of pet loss and as a celebration of your pet's life. Creating a video series that showcases your pet's quirks, lessons they taught you, and how they changed your life can also be a powerful way to connect with others and extend the influence of your pet's love. These narratives not only keep your pet's memory alive but also help others feel less alone in their grief, fostering a community of support and understanding.

Whether through community service, personal acts of love, or story-telling, you are building a legacy of love that honors your pet. This legacy is a dynamic tribute, continuously evolving and growing as you find new ways to express the depth of the bond you shared. It ensures that the love, joy, and lessons your pet brought into your life continue to resonate and influence, touching lives and making the world a slightly better place, just as your pet did for you. Through these living legacies, we not only keep our cherished pets' memories alive but also amplify the love they showed us, passing it on in countless meaningful ways.

Embracing Joy and Remembrance: The Path Forward

The echoes of a bark or the soft purr that once filled your home can stir a profound sense of loss, yet within these memories lies a treasure trove of joy waiting to be rediscovered. As you navigate the waters of remembrance, transforming your perspective on these memories from sources of pain to cherished treasures can profoundly impact your emotional healing. Each playful jump, each lazy afternoon, and each loving nuzzle is a snapshot of joy that, when remembered, can bring a smile as readily as it might bring a tear. Embrace these memories with gratitude as each one is a testament to the love and bond you shared with your pet. Allow yourself to bask in the warmth of these moments, letting them fill your heart with the joy and love that characterized your time together.

Encouraging the celebration of your pet's life is equally vital. Focus on organizing events or moments that highlight the happiness you shared. This could be an annual gathering in your pet's favorite park, where friends and family can come together to share stories and celebrate the pet's life. Alternatively, creating a digital photo album that showcases the best moments you shared and sharing it online can not only help you revisit these joyful times but also allow others to appreciate the beauty and happiness of your pet's life. Celebrating these moments underscores the positive impact your pet had on your life and helps shift the narrative from one of loss to one of appreciation and celebration.

Furthermore, remembering your pet should not solely be a source of sadness but can also be a profound source of joy and strength. Setting aside a special day to celebrate your pet's life, perhaps on their birthday or the day they came into your life, can be a powerful tradition. On this day, engage in activities that you enjoyed together, or donate to an animal charity in their name, turning your remembrance into positive action that benefits others. Such acts keep the memory of your pet alive in a dynamic and joyful way, helping to reinforce the positive aspects of their life and the time you shared.

The journey of grief and love is indeed ongoing and deeply intertwined. It's a delicate dance of remembering and moving forward, where both emotions coexist and inform each other. Acknowledge that it is perfectly normal to feel joy and sadness simultaneously. As you continue to embrace the memories and celebrate the life of your beloved pet, allow yourself to feel all the nuances of these emotions without judgment. This open-hearted approach ensures that the love you shared with your pet continues to grow within you, influencing your life and actions in positive, meaningful ways. By accepting this ongoing process, you affirm that love, once rooted in your heart, does not fade; it evolves and accompanies you every day, guiding and inspiring you as you move forward.

In embracing both the joy and remembrance of your pet, you forge a path that honors their memory while actively engaging with the love they left behind. This approach not only helps heal the heart but also enriches your life with a deeper appreciation of the bonds we share with our animal companions. As you continue to navigate this path, let the joy and love you rediscovered in your memories light your way, turning the pain of loss into a celebration of life and an ongoing journey of love.

Conclusion

As we reach the closing pages of our shared journey, I invite you to pause and reflect on the path we have journeyed through together. From the raw, initial waves of grief to the gradual steps toward healing and remembrance. The transformation you've experienced may not always have been easy, but it has been significant, and it's important to acknowledge the courage it has taken to move through each stage.

Throughout this book, we've delved into the profound bond shared between pets and their owners, understanding that the loss of such a beloved companion triggers a deep and legitimate form of grief. We've explored the stages of grief, offering practical coping strategies and ways to support not just ourselves but also our children and other family members. We've discussed how to memorialize our pets in meaningful ways and how these acts of remembrance can help us cope with loss. Most importantly, we've looked at finding resilience and joy after loss, emphasizing that the pain of grief can eventually give way to the celebration of love shared.

The significance of validating pet loss cannot be overstated. Recognizing this form of grief is crucial, as it allows us to seek and offer support in ways that acknowledge the true depth of our emotional bonds with our pets. Remember, your journey through grief is uniquely yours, and it unfolds at its own pace. Embrace this path without judgment, and allow yourself the space and time to heal.

I encourage you to keep using the coping strategies, memorial practices, and support systems we've discussed. Adapt them over time to fit your changing needs and continue to find comfort and strength in the memories of your beloved pet. There is hope in every story, and continuity in every end. Your journey of healing can inspire acts of kindness, spur community involvement, or motivate personal growth all in honor of the love and lessons your pet brought into your life.

I invite you to share your own stories of pet loss, healing, and remembrance with others. Whether it's with friends, family, or through online communities, sharing can deepen connections and provide support to those who walk this path alongside you. Your strength and resilience in facing this grief head-on are commendable, and I thank you deeply for trusting this book to be a part of your healing process.

As we part ways, I leave you with this thought: How can you keep the love and memory of your pet alive in your daily actions? Remember, love never truly leaves us; it only transforms into new ways of being and connecting.

Thank you once again for allowing me to accompany you on this journey. May you find peace and joy in the love that you and your pet shared, and may you continue to carry that love forward in every step you take.

With warmth and solidarity,

Xydnee James

Call To Help

I hope you truly enjoyed the book and found it's contents informative and useful. As an author our words can only go as far as the message we bring is delivered so we're asking you for help. Please help us share this message of hope, support, and comfort to others who are experiencing the pain of losing a pet. I ask that you would write an Amazon review for this book to help others find solace, guidance, and support via this book. If you're up to the challenge, please scan the QR code below so you can write your review.

References

- *7 Benefits of Being an Animal Shelter Volunteer* https://ccs pca.com/blog-spca/benefits-animal-shelter-volunteer/

- *7 Ways To Support Your Spouse As They Grieve The Loss* ... https://counselorforcouples.com/7-ways-to-support-yo ur-spouse-as-they-grieve-the-loss-of-a-pet/

- *12 special pet memorial service ideas* https://www.betterpla ceforests.com/blog/12-special-pet-memorial-service-ideas/

- *Can Physical Activity Support Grief Outcomes in Individuals* ... https://www.ncbi.nlm.nih.gov/pmc/articles/PMC8028 581/

- *Coping with Losing a Pet* https://www.helpguide.org/artic les/grief/coping-with-losing-a-pet.htm

- *Coping with the loss of a pet* https://www.avma.org/resourc es-tools/pet-owners/petcare/coping-loss-pet

- *Create the Perfect Pet Memorial Gar- den* https://perfectmemorials.com/guides/create-the-perfe ct-pet-memorial-garden/

- *Death of Pets: Talking to Children - AACAP* https://www.aacap.org/AACAP/Families_and_Youth/Fac ts_for_Families/FFF-Guide/When-A-Pet-Dies-078.aspx

- *Dog Memorial Ideas: 10 Ways to Honor Your Dog's Legacy* https://toegrips.com/dog-memorial-ideas/

- *History and Science of the Human-Animal Bond* https://todaysveterinarynurse.com/personal-professional-d evelopment/history-and-science-of-the-human-animal-bon d/

- *How Journaling Can Help You Grieve* https://www.psychologytoday.com/us/blog/understandin g-grief/202101/how-journaling-can-help-you-grieve

- *How Losing a Pet Can Make You Stronger* https://www.nytimes.com/2021/05/03/health/p ets-death-lessons-strength.html

- *How to help a grieving dog* https://www.bluecross.org.uk/a dvice/dog/how-to-help-a-grieving-dog

- *How to Plan a Pet Memorial Service* https://www.furevermemorials.com/pet-loss/how-to -plan-a-pet-memorial-service/

- *Life Expectancy of Dogs and Cats | PetMed- s®* https://www.1800petmeds.com/education/life-expecta ncy-dog-cat-40.html

- *The Association for Pet Loss and Bereave- ment* https://www.samhsa.gov/resource/dbhis/association

-pet-loss-bereavement

- *The Benefits of Having a Memorial Service for Your Pet* https://www.jeffersonmemorial.com/about-us/news/the-benefits-of-having-a-memorial-service-for-your-pet

- *The Impact of Continuing Bonds Between Pet Owners and ...* https://journals.sagepub.com/doi/full/10.1177/00302228221125955

- *Unique Pet Memorial Ideas* https://www.myfarewelling.com/article/pet-memorial-ideas

- Vinehall School - Play is serious learning. https://www.vinehallschool.com/blog/?pid=11&nid=5&storyid=39

- *Ways to Memorialize Your Pet - UF Small Animal Hospital* https://smallanimal.vethospital.ufl.edu/resources/pet-loss-support/ways-to-memorialize-your-pet/

- *When a Pet Dies: Helping Kids Cope (for Parents)* https://kidshealth.org/en/parents/pet-death.html

- *When a Pet Dies: How to Help Your Child Cope* https://www.healthychildren.org/English/healthy-living/emotional-wellness/Building-Resilience/Pages/when-a-pet-dies-how-to-help-your-child-cope.aspx

- *When Is It the Right Time for a New Pet?* https://www.lapoflove.com/blog/pet-loss-support/when-is-the-right-time-for-a-new-pet

- Wikipedia contributors. (n.d.). *Five stages of grief.*

Wikipedia, The Free Encyclopedia. Retrieved May 19, 2024,

f   r   o   m

https://en.wikipedia.org/wiki/Five_stages_of_grief#:~:text
=According%20to%20the%20model%20of,%2C%20bargai
ning%2C%20depression%20and%20acceptance